PROUST AND THE SENSE OF TIME

PROUST

AND THE SENSE OF TIME

Julia Kristeva

Translated and with an Introduction by
STEPHEN BANN

Columbia University Press
New York

First published in 1993 by
Columbia University Press, New York
and in Great Britain by Faber and Faber Limited

Copyright © 1993 Julia Kristeva
English translation © 1993 Stephen Bann

Library of Congress Cataloging-in-Publication Data
Kristeva, Julia, 1941–
Proust and the sense of time/Julia Kristeva: translated and
with an introduction by Stephen Bann.
p.   cm.
Includes bibliographical references and index.
ISBN 0–231–08478–1
1. Proust, Marcel, 1871–1922. A la recherche du temps perdu.
2. Psychoanalysis and literature.   3. Time in literature.
I. Title.
PQ2631.R63A8273   1993
843'.912—dc20
93–19359
CIP

Phototypeset by Wilmaset Ltd, Wirral, England
Printed in England by Clays Ltd, St Ives plc

C 10 9 8 7 6 5 4 3 2 1

Contents

Foreword

The publication of these four lectures marks an event both in Proust studies, and in the development of Julia Kristeva's remarkable career as a writer and critic. It is, to begin with, the first time that she has written at any length on the writer who, more than any other contemporary French figure, has been naturalized within the canon of modern English literature. It is also the first time that the initial fruits of her research in such an important field have been presented, before French publication, to the English reader.

Proust imposed a heavy burden of anxiety on his critics by being himself a critic of exceptional subtlety and penetration. Moreover, his message in *Against Sainte-Beuve*, reiterated across the vast canvas of *A la recherche du temps perdu*, is that criticism frequently makes the vulgar error of confusing the interest attached to the work with the incidental information to be derived from studying the author's biography. Even if the narrator is at first fascinated by the thought of meeting Bergotte face to face, he soon learns that the beauty of Bergotte's texts and the insignificant impression created by their author have nothing in common.

As if in accord with this warning, much of the outstanding Proust criticism of recent years has been rhetorical in character, reminiscent of Proust's meticulous dissection of 'Flaubert's style' (see *Against Sainte-Beuve*, pp. 261–74).

Hardly had George Painter started to issue his lengthy biographical study in 1959 than Gérard Genette began his scrupulous and sensitive investigations into Proust's use of figurative language with 'Proust Palimpsest'. Genette's work culminated in 1972 with his essay on 'Metonymy in Proust' and his comprehensive study of the narrative structures of *A la recherche*, translated into English as *Narrative Discourse*.

When reading Genette we get the sense that *A la recherche* is a kind of absolute text. It is hardly necessary to stray beyond its boundaries to find every possible feature of the narrator's repertoire. This sense of Proust as a paragon of textual practice has by no means diminished as structural and rhetorical analysis has yielded to post-structuralism. Paul de Man employs Proust in *Allegories of Reading* to demonstrate the fissure between grammar and rhetoric, and its consequences for the undecidability of meaning. In a recent article, 'The Rhetoric of Interpretation', Hayden White has brilliantly analysed the passage describing the fountain in the courtyard of the Hôtel de Guermantes, and arrives at the firm conclusion that Proust's narrative is 'an allegory of figuration itself'.

It almost seems as though Proust succeeded only too well in deflecting his critics from wishing to assert any hard and fast connection between experience and the text. In this respect, of course, his prescriptions have been powerfully seconded more recently by the critical strategy of Roland Barthes, especially in his widely read essays 'From Work to Text' and 'The Death of the Author'. Barthes rarely wrote about Proust. But the effect of his work on Proust studies can easily be detected if we take Leslie Hill's fine 'Proust and the Art of Reading'. If, for Barthes, the death of the author implies the birth of a new type of reader, then this reader (in Hill's terms) could hardly do better than test the new skills on the Proustian text.

There is one substantial exception to this rule of text-based and reader-orientated criticism of Proust, and this comes into view through what Kristeva herself terms the 'magnificent reading' of Gilles Deleuze. First published in 1964, Deleuze's *Proust and Signs* is indeed an extraordinary achievement: it portrays the enterprise of *A la recherche* as a quest, in which the would-be author learns progressively to decipher and ultimately to disregard the signs of worldliness and the signs of love, reaching the illuminating conclusion that the signs of art alone offer a kind of fulfilment. Is Deleuze writing about Proust the biographical subject, or about the narrator Marcel? In a sense, this crucial issue for literary critics is put in suspension by Deleuze's approach. As a philosopher and historian of ideas himself, Deleuze unquestionably implies that it is Proust, and not his *persona* Marcel, who is engaged in the acquisition of wisdom through the understanding of art.

Julia Kristeva's place in this debate has been established in advance by the development of her own critical approach over more than a quarter of a century. Although her first contribution to French intellectual life came within the framework of a lively interest in Russian formalism during the 1960s, her focus on the work of Bakhtin indicated precisely the necessity to go beyond formalism. As she wrote in the Introduction to the French translation of *Dostoevsky* (1970): 'Bakhtin surveys a continent which the instruments of poetics cannot attain.' Bakhtin's message for the contemporary critic was therefore categorical: it was to entail 'a search for those rules by which the meaning and its speaker are brought into being, and which the extremist texts of our time have been the first to produce'.

Thus the programme was already announced in 1970. But the method of achieving it could not, at that stage, have been predicted. Kristeva's investigation of the genesis of meaning took on, as a result of her simultaneous investigation of linguistics and psychoanalysis, the character of a search for a theory of the subject. But as this subject could be understood only as the product of more than two millennia of historical and cultural evolution, it also became an exercise in the historical retrieval of the conditions of subjectivity. Whereas Derrida applied himself to the deconstruction of the Western metaphysical tradition – largely assimilated to the legacy of Plato – Kristeva pursued an alternative strategy, in which, while the Greeks were not neglected, the major exegetic effort went into the reconstruction of Judaic law and Christian theology. It is more than probable that, in this objective, she was aided by the lapidary hints of Lacan, and the speculations of René Girard, whose achievement she was one of the first to salute. But the historical and psychological illuminations offered by such books as *Powers of Horror* and *Tales of Love* remain distinctively her own.

How, then, does this track lead to Proust? It goes without saying that his work cannot be classed among 'the extremist texts of our time'. Indeed these lectures will show how comprehensively Kristeva places French writing of the last fifty years, for all its merits, within the shadow of Proust: its 'extremism', when measured against the uniquely capacious character of *A la recherche*, amounts in fact to a fragment-ation. It is almost as if Proust had to be approached through history – that is to say, through the genealogical stages of subjectivity which Kristeva has systematically traced – rather than through the inadequate grid of 'modernism', or 'con-temporary literature'. Set against the background of the Western tradition, he achieves an absolute, unchallenged status: not simply as the author of a text which demonstrates the most virtuoso use of the possibilities of language, but also as the sage who reconciles a penetrating knowledge of the social world with an intimate devotion to the enrichment of the inner life through the medium of time.

Does this mean the return of the biographical subject? In a sense, it undoubtedly does. But this is not the lugubrious, mustachioed figure of Painter's study, who steers his way through a cast of insubstantial characters only to conflate them, with admirable economy, into the chief actors of his fiction. Kristeva is so far from wishing to endorse the view of Proust as a snobbish, shallow character – who somehow achieved the alchemy of great art – that she insists (like Deleuze and Girard) on his position of objectivity *vis-à-vis* the society he describes. Where Girard contrasts the narcissistic hero of *Jean Santeuil* with the narrator who has learned to view the brilliance of the Guermantes at a distance, Kristeva traces the development of a similar motif from the early, unfinished essay on Chardin to the frightening image of the X-ray operator towards the end of *A la recherche*. Like the X-ray operator, the artist scrutinizes his subject only to find the disease that is gnawing away at it internally. Like Deleuze's initiate, Kristeva's Proust learns to put away worldly things.

No less important, Kristeva insists on the whole dimension of Proust's experience which constitutes his relation to maternity. Picking up Georges Bataille's suggestive thoughts on the 'profanation of the mother', she explores the deep sado-masochistic impulses which can be detected both in Proust's writings and in the reported details of his life. Through examining the exact chronology of the different drafts involved in the preparation of *A la recherche*, she is able to put forward a concrete and plausible hypothesis about the way in which Mme Proust's death figured in the gradual, progressive transformation of the decadent, dandified young writer into the creator of *A la recherche*.

Maternity also dominates the analysis which Kristeva offers

of the most celebrated, and cliché-ridden, of all the episodes in the novel: the incident involving the madeleine at the end of Proust's *Overture*. This close reading of a relatively brief text is, in fact, the clearest evidence of the new and invigorating reading which Kristeva brings to Proust. There is no disputing that, from the rhetorical point of view, the *Overture* could be viewed as a cascade of metaphors and metonymies, establishing the structures along which the narrative will move. But Kristeva portrays it as a specific sequence of subjective stages, in which the madeleine is used to prefigure the challenge of a mother's love that is initially intolerable, but can be tamed and objectified through cunning displacements. Inevitably, this mode of reading draws upon the details of Proust's personal life, and the role of Céleste Albaret, as his faithful housekeeper, is seen as the culminating factor in Proust's mature creativity: writer and housekeeper unite in the cult of 'the good mother'.

Kristeva's approach is certainly not to repudiate the achievements of recent Proust criticism, but to indicate none the less, as often as possible, the ways in which Proust eludes and exceeds normative expectations. In looking carefully at the role of metaphor in his work, she does not dispute the conclusions of Ullmann and Genette, but insists at the same time on the philosophical weight which Proust attaches to the metaphorical process: for Proust, the essence of metaphor is expressed by a relationship of analogy, and 'the analogical is the ontological'. Equally, though she respects the originality of Deleuze's study, she does not accept the crucial assumption that Proust's discussion of 'being', 'idea' and 'essence' has to be seen within the tradition of Platonic metaphysics. On the contrary, she carefully assesses recent research into the philosophical milieu which the young Proust knew, and concludes that he framed his philosophical notions in response to the example of the French disciples of Schopenhauer. This hard evidence is far more worthwhile than the frequently proffered conjectural evidence about Proust's debt to Bergson, and it succeeds in showing that, in his social thought as well, Proust benefited from his well-planned philosophical education.

Yet it is not as a contribution to the history of ideas that Kristeva's work on Proust deserves to be recorded. Something more radical is involved in her strategy of recalling 'experience' to the centre of critical focus, and of setting up Proust as the touchstone of an adequate contemporary theory of literature. That Proust understood our own period, as well as his own, is explicitly asserted here. Sartre spent the last years of his life pondering the enigma of Flaubert who, in his view, sacrificed his life in order to gain the immortality of authorship – a bargain which Sartre can respect, but in no way endorse. For Kristeva, the magnitude of Proust's sacrifices in the interests of the work should not be minimized. But we would do well to take his achievement not as a bizarre object-lesson, but as a guide to psychic survival.

Stephen Bann
July 1992

Note on the translation

Except where indicated by a reference, all passages quoted from *A la recherche du temps perdu* have been taken from the current English edition, translated by Terence Kilmartin (Marcel Proust, *Remembrance of Things Past*, 3 vols, Penguin Classics, Harmondsworth, 1985). Quotations are identified by volume and page number from this edition. In a few cases, the wording has been slightly altered to follow the nuances of the critical argument.

Proust's major work is referred to throughout this text as *A la recherche*. Titles of individual parts are cited in the style used by the Penguin edition, except where these revert to Scott Moncrieff's rather figurative choices (e.g. *Sodom and Gomorrah* is used rather than *Cities of the Plain*).

The following abbreviations are also used to identify particular editions in the text and in the references:

ALR Marcel Proust, *A la recherche du temps perdu*, 4 vols, ed. Jean-Yves Tadié *et al.* (Gallimard, Bibliothèque de la Pléiade, 1987–9)

CSB Marcel Proust, *Contre Sainte-Beuve*, ed. Pierre Clarac (Gallimard, Bibliothèque de la Pléiade, 1971)

ASB Marcel Proust, *Against Sainte-Beuve and Other Essays*, trans. John Sturrock (London, Penguin, 1988)

Preface

Eliot's work and Eliot's genius, which provide the occasion for this series of Memorial Lectures, have always fascinated me. The attention he devotes to sensuality, in particular where it involves human distress and the abject side of the human condition; the interest he takes in new forms of critical discourse; his style, which varies between the concise and the exuberant; his insistence on the need to renew spiritual values without losing touch with tradition; his European mentality – all of these aspects will remain at the back of my mind as I deliver these lectures.

As far as Proust is concerned, you will know better than I Eliot's admiration for this great French writer. The lectures by Bergson which Eliot followed at the Sorbonne are by no means the only link between them. You will probably be able to conclude as the week goes on that there are much deeper connections. To begin with, I will touch upon a few striking facts, very briefly, in order to make the transition to my reflections on the work of Proust, where I feel myself more at home.

As the young editor of *The Criterion* magazine Eliot published in April 1924 the remarkable article by Ernst Robert Curtius, translated from the German, 'On the Style of Marcel Proust'. In July 1924 he published 'The Death of Albertine', in Scott Moncrieff's translation. When he wrote the Preface to the reissue of *The Criterion* in 1967, he pointed out: 'I am proud to have introduced to English readers the work of Marcel Proust.'[1]

In addition, the new edition of the *Letters* of Eliot edited by Mrs Valerie Eliot demonstrates that in 1922 Eliot was extremely anxious to make contact with Proust and to publish one of his texts in English. In a letter to Ezra Pound, dated 9 July 1922, he wrote: 'I am *not* anxious to get many French people for the *first two* numbers . . . the only name worth getting is *Proust*, whom I am fishing for.'[2] In a letter of 6 November 1922, he refers to the Curtius article, and assures his correspondent that Proust himself very much approves of it ('an essay . . . which Proust is highly pleased with').[3]

I hope my commentaries on the experience of Proust will demonstrate to you the extent of this affinity between Eliot and the author of *A la recherche*, which implies something more than mere cultural politics, but rather a number of deep similarities.

I
PROUST AND
TIME EMBODIED

———————

I

Time and timelessness

Marcel Proust (1871–1922) composed *A la recherche du temps perdu* between 1913 (the year of the publication of *Du côté de chez Swann* by Grasset) and 1922. The last volume, *Le Temps retrouvé*, published like its predecessors by Gallimard, was to appear in 1927. Proust is often seen as being closer in spirit to the symbolists, dandies and assorted decadents of the *fin de siècle* than to the sardonic and playful activities of the dadaists, surrealists and futurists propagated by the First World War, not to mention the nightmarish cult of the absurd which followed the Second. Yet it was this man of the nineteenth century who inaugurated the modern aesthetic, and established a completely new form of temporality. Its function is to sum up, and make explicit, the ambitions of all the novels that have gone before, through creating a distinctively new type of *Bildungsroman* (the German genre which deals with the hero's education and intellectual development); in this case the learning process involves a return journey from the past to the present and back again. This new form of temporality, furthermore, gives an X-ray image of memory, bringing to light its painful yet rapturous dependence on the senses. It offers modern readers the chance to identify the fragments of disparate time which are nowadays dragging them in every direction, with a greater force and insistence than ever before.

So I would like to begin by putting a question to you, and to myself as well. What is the time-scale that you belong to? What is the time that you speak from? In the modern world, you might catch an impression of the medieval Inquisition from a nationalist dictator who soon finished spreading the message of integration. (I refer to the Gulf War.) Then you might be rejuvenated by 150 or 200 years by a Victorian president whose stiff, puritanical attitudes belong to the great age of the Protestant conquest of the New World, tempered by an eighteenth-century regard for human rights. But you are also an onlooker, even if you are not a participant, when people demonstrate their regression to infancy through civil violence, as in the recent events in Los Angeles; you witness the futurist breakthroughs of new musical forms like rap, without for a moment forgetting the wise explanatory discourses with which the newspapers and the universities try to explain this sort of thing. Newspapers and universities, by the way, continuing their role of transmitting and handing down knowledge, also belong to totally different time-scales. Yes, we live in a dislocated chronology, and there is as yet no concept that will make sense of this modern, dislocated experience of temporality.

Psychic time as a space of reconciliation

Living on the threshold of this disturbing epoch, Proust managed to put together the shattered fragments in the form of the life of his narrator, who experiences love and society in accordance with a number of themes which we may think of as archaic, but are in fact our very own, because of their polarized and discontinuous logic. For Proust, time is to be psychic time, and consequently the factor which determines our bodily life. I will argue that time in fact persists as the only surviving imaginative value which can be used by the novel to appeal to the whole community of readers.

Things come to have meaning when the I of the writer rediscovers the sensations underlying them, which are always linked together in at least a series of two (as in the case of the madeleine offered to me by my mother and the one offered by Aunt Léonie; the paving stones of the Guermantes courtyard and those at St Mark's, Venice). Time is this bringing together of two sensations which gush out from the signs and signal themselves to me. But since bringing things together is a *metaphor*, and sensation implies a *body*, Proustian time, which brings together the sensations imprinted in signs, is a *metamorphosis*. It is all too easy to rely on just one word of the title and conclude that this is a novel about time. Proust uses time as his intermediary *in the search* (*A la recherche*) for an embodied imagination: that is to say, for a space where words and their dark, unconscious manifestations contribute to the weaving of the world's unbroken flesh, of which I is a part. I as writer; I as reader; I living, loving and dying.

From Homer to Balzac, fiction creates and modifies its own destiny by offering those who receive it a special field of participation, a distinctive type of communion: it shows us human passions inextricably bound up with the unpredictability of nature and the harshnesses of society. Man, society and being are, for fiction, indissociable. Hence over the period from Rabelais and Shakespeare to Balzac, fiction has blended the serious with the ridiculous, and managed to extract from its chosen area the idea of a time which is specific to the individual – this so-called modern individual whose inner life, in all its different phases of sorrow, joy or ridicule, weaves its own form of continuity which is the thread of a destiny.

Proust in no way abandons the ambition of Balzac and Homer – which is sociological in an explicit way, but conceals a transcendental aim at its basis. He is concerned to establish a world in which his readers can come and communicate as if they were in a sacred place: a world where they can discover a coherence between time and space and their dreams can be realized, a place which is sadly lacking in modern reality. His Faubourg Saint-Germain (which in fact corresponds more closely to the Faubourg Saint-Honoré) fulfils this aim of establishing a social space, which is the very definition of the sacred in literature. Here it is, majestic as it approaches its demise, glorious and at the same time ridiculous, no less desirable in the first pages of the opening volumes than it will be perverted and intolerable by the final stage, when we see the very impulse that brought it into being by claiming to draw inspiration from it come full circle in the concept of a *Temps retrouvé* (*Time Regained*). From the start, social life is offered as a spectacle. We must not take our eyes off it, but we can overtake it by a strategy that enables us to pass far beyond the social; this strategy consists in delving deep down into ourselves, in regaining the time of our inner lives, which has been so subtly reordered that this time now comes to seem the only reality worth taking into account.

So Proust does not relinquish the obsession of authors from Homer to Balzac. But he tones it down by linking it with a project which traditionally belongs to 'poetry': this is the exploration of memory, with the 'I' unfolding ideas and images, recalling flavours, smells, touches, resonances, sensations, jealousies, exasperations, griefs and joys – if it succeeds in articulating them. But to the extent that he offers us *the space of memory* as a residual area of value leading beyond the spectacle of worldly life in its drama, Proust also aligns himself with a tendency of philosophy contemporary with him: one which, from Bergson to Heidegger, in different ways but with significant points in common, seeks to understand Being by exploring the obscurities of Time. Proust goes further indeed, since he puts into words a category of *felt time* which cuts through the categories of metaphysics, bringing together opposites like idea, duration and space, on the one hand, and force, perception, emotion and desire, on the other; he proposes a psychic universe of the maximum degree of complexity as the favourable location – the place of sacred communion – where lovers of reading can meet.

Do we want tales of passion? Of money? Of war? Of life and death? Without any doubt, we have enough in Proust to keep up with the official statistics. But this is something quite different. If you will only be so good as to open up your memories of felt time, *there* will rise the new cathedral. Upon the plinth of a project which is by tradition secular and dates back to the Greeks, Proust's novel sets up a huge edifice which has instead a biblical and evangelical provenance. And within this network of interminable social events, of endless plots, plots and more plots, he situates a person, *I*, a subject whose memory cannot be impugned, who is there to bring out the convulsive truth of this seeming history, to 'tear off its hundred masks'. *I* invites you to do as *I* does. *Read me, and you will be part of the world but without being taken in by it. I can give you the Divine Comedy of the life of the psyche, not just mine, but yours as well, ours, that is, the absolute.*

In creating this synthesis, in using memory to construct *A la recherche* in this way, Proust is adopting an ethical position. He is contrasting the disarray of the world and of the self with the unending search for that lost temple, that invisible temple, which is *the felt time of our subjective memories*. In taking up his aesthetic stance, he is also adopting a moral position *vis-à-vis* the cult of decadence, which he has passed through and, to a great extent, emerged from; Proust is a moralist therefore, but he is a moralist of outrage. The felt time in which he invites us to participate is one of sensual excess and extravagant eroticism, of ruses and betrayals. His sacredness is a sacredness of ill repute. In bringing it to light with the delicate touches of a Saint-Simon or a Mme de Sévigné, Proust the dandy of the *belle époque* makes contact with us in our contemporary, but also timeless, obsessions. There have been many people, since Proust, who have applied themselves to enlarging a fragment of felt time – writers of the *nouveau roman* have enhanced such fragments as if they were installing them in a stained-glass window. They may appear to be more modern, more elliptical, provocative and 'transgressive'. But Proust remains the only one to keep the balance between the violence implicit in the marginal status of the main character (and the author) of *A la recherche*, and the graceful capacity for creating a world, a place of communion in worldly time. It is this fragile balance that we seem to have lost. Perhaps that is another reason why Proust, our contemporary, is also so difficult to reach in his intimate life.

Plants and seeds: the vocation

Proust's notebooks, and his *Against Sainte-Beuve* (composed between 1905 and 1909), tell us that the plan of *A la recherche* was fixed by 1908–9. The eventual text proceeds through successive alterations and adjustments between 1909 and 1911; then from 1916 onwards we see the final manuscript notebooks emerging. These had not yet been typed out at the time of Proust's death in 1922. In a letter dated 16 August 1908, he confesses to Mme Straus:

I have just begun, and finished, a whole book. Unfortunately, leaving for Cabourg has interrupted my work. I am just about to get back to it. Maybe part of it will appear in serial form in *Le Figaro*, but only part of it, for it is too long and unsuitable to be published in its entirety. But I do want to finish it, to make an end. Everything is written down, but there is a lot to go over again.[1]

'Unsuitable', 'long' – Proust already knows how his work will begin and end, and what will be its chief features – its outrageous contents and its disproportionate style. The First World War and his illness would delay and modify his original plan: Proust evidently could not have been aware in 1909 of the various changes that would be introduced in the course of time. But the central scheme – the approach and the 'vision', as he would later refer to it when speaking of his style – are already in place. In the cork-lined bedroom on the Boulevard Haussmann, in the month of July 1909, there begins the metamorphosis of *Against Sainte-Beuve* into that starting point of *A la recherche* which will be *Du côté de chez Swann* (*Swann's Way*). Notebook 3, which dates from this stage, actually contains eight versions of the narrator's famous awakening scene – his mind invaded by formless sensations seeming to come from an adjacent room, just before the appearance of the familiar sounds and lights will bring him to full consciousness.[2] 'Involuntary memory' is already there, causing the boiling lava of memories and desires from the past to coagulate around a present sensation, however slight, however intense.

So what has been happening between the commencement of *Against Sainte-Beuve* and the emergence of this fully fledged project – between 1905 and 1909?

2

The dead mother

At the end of *Time Regained*, after bringing up yet again the way in which the narrator's experience is structured by the alternation of love and death, with death darkening love but love wiping out the fear of death, Proust quotes a line from Victor Hugo: 'The grass must grow and children have to die.'[3] And he describes the 'cruel law of art' which amounts in the first instance to the romantic notion that suffering and death are necessary for the gestation of works of art, but concludes with a light-hearted apologia for Manet, considered as the Giorgione of a period of open-air painting:

To me it seems more correct to say that the cruel law of art is that people die and we ourselves die after exhausting every form of suffering, so that over our heads may grow the grass not of oblivion but of eternal life, the vigorous and luxuriant growth of a true work of art, and so that thither, gaily and without a thought for those who are sleeping beneath them, future generations may come to enjoy their *déjeuner sur l'herbe*. (III. 1095)

In this context, it is Albertine who is the object of so much love and so much jealousy. It is her accidental and premature death which has detached the narrator from sexual desire in the same measure as it has made him indifferent to death, and has entrenched him all the more securely within another reality: that of 'my book'.

The vigorous and luxuriant grass of the work requires a

death. A child's death? And if so, which child? Albertine? Or
the narrator himself, who has died many times, so he believes,
since his childhood: dying at every parting, every separation,
every bedtime which tears him away from his parents, from
his mummy? And what if the child remained in existence only
as long as there was a mother there? In that event, the mother
would have to die in order for the child to break with his
childhood, for him to turn it into a memory, a time regained.
Were he finally to regain all his time, set out in the space of a
book, then the book would indeed be a '*déjeuner sur l'herbe*':
it would transform the graveyard of the dead children into a
pleasure garden, dedicated to the ambiguous, loving and
vengeful memory of a mother who always loved excessively
and not enough – and made you into a child who is still dying,
perhaps, but who has a chance of ultimate resurrection and
maturity in the luxuriant grass of the book.

Mme Proust, née Jeanne-Clemence Weil, died on 26
September 1905, following a short visit to Evian with her son
Marcel, in the course of which, while staying at the Hôtel
Splendide, she suffered an attack of uraemia. The sudden
illness and death agony of the narrator's grandmother in *A la
recherche du temps perdu* recall the remorse felt by Proust as a
result of his feeble behaviour at this juncture. Mme Proust first
asked to be photographed, hesitated, and later called it off:
'She wanted and she didn't want to be photographed, wishing
to leave me one last image, and yet afraid that it would be too
distressing . . .'⁴ A collector of photographs, Proust would
later put his family snapshots to blasphemous use, showing
them around at the Le Cuziat brothel.

On her return to the Rue de Courcelles, the dying woman
could think only of her elder son. How would he survive
without her? She died while Proust stayed alone in his room,
unable to cope with the sight of his mother's death agony.

There is no event that can explain the genesis of a work, not even the death of a woman like Mme Proust. The book had been maturing for ages, yet it was mourning his mother that marked the start of a new time-scale and a new way of life. 'Since I lost my mother . . .' Proust often refers to the event in his correspondence, and he does not attempt to hide his wounds in his letters to Montesquiou, Barrès and Maurice Duplay.[5] The second volume of *Le Côté de Guermantes (The Guermantes Way*; 1921) continually harps on the illness, suffering and finally death agony of the narrator's grandmother, as if intending to lend to salon life, which the young man finds attractive and empty by turns, an unreal and hallucinatory quality. Yet it is in *Sodome et Gomorrhe* (*Sodom and Gomorrah*), published in 1921 and 1922, that the note of black remorse, anticipated in the earlier works, finally strikes home. This is the novel of sexual inversion, no less distinct from the childhood memories of *Swann's Way* than it is from the aesthetic theory of *Time Regained*. It is in this work, which has been called the most Balzacian of the series, that Proust makes the clearest allusion, in the form of allusions to the death of the narrator's grandmother, to the sense of guilt brought about by his mother's death.

As the years go on, and the work progresses with them, the scenes of sexual inversion occupy a more and more important place. Albertine's lesbianism is the major stimulus for the blend of jealousy and fascination which the narrator feels for this young woman. Society figures, not excluding the irreproachable Prince de Guermantes, turn out to have perverse habits. The adventures of Charlus with Jupien and Morel reach a high point of moral and physical cruelty, culminating in the flagellation scene in the brothel. This homosexual, explicitly erotic *mise-en-scène* becomes possible only in *Sodom and Gomorrah*, and in it the vision which we can now appreciate to be the real kernel of Proust's imaginary world, its 'albumen' and 'seed', crystallizes. *The sado-masochism of Sodom and Gomorrah is the truth underlying eroticism and feeling and, on a deeper level, sado-masochism is the very bond that brings society together.*

A crucial episode

The inclusion, in a section entitled 'The Intermittencies of the Heart', of the (grand-)mother's death gives the narrator the chance not only to recall childhood memories (his boots and his dressing-gown), but also to discourse at length on two of the fundamental themes of *A la recherche*. On the one hand, the joyful experience of passion is invariably accompanied by a sense of the nothingness, the mortality and the foreign nature of the loved one, a combination which engenders delightful forms of suffering. On the other hand, the faculty of memory which reveals this exquisite duality to us is lodged in an 'unknown domain', 'in the entire existence of our bodies', with the effect that 'a series of different and parallel' states of the self are superimposed, and consequently the self of today can rediscover the previous self intact, provided that the underlying sensations have the character of 'intermittencies': being both violent enough and null at the same time, tender and listless, combining joy with grief and remorse:

For with the *perturbations of memory* are linked the *intermittencies of the heart* . . . But if the context of sensations in which they are preserved is recaptured, they acquire in turn the same power of expelling everything that is incompatible with them, of installing alone in us the self that originally lived them . . . *without any solution of continuity*, immediately after the first evening at Balbec long ago . . . I clung to the minute in which my grandmother had stooped over me. The self that I then was, that had disappeared for so long, was once again so close to me that I seemed still to hear the words that had just been spoken, although they were now no more than a phantasm . . . (II.784) [my italics]

My commentary on this extract is that we are offered a foretaste of memory as comprising the successive states of the self, and of time regained, even to the very sensations: the narrator experiences grief, ecstasy and even indifference in unison with the dramas of sexuality to be made manifest by the two biblical cities. This implies that the (grand-)mother's death makes it possible for violence and remorse to be inserted into the very heart of the child-narrator's sensibility, and at the same time it is implied that cruelty is omnipresent, even in the purity of childhood. Time will be truly regained only if he rediscovers the particular form of violence – the violence that is, initially, one of archaic loss and vengeance. That which delights me and abandons me also kills me; but I am capable of putting to death that which is my delight.

Yet in this crucial year, 1905, when Proust has already anticipated and indeed sketched out the theme of inversion (in *Jean Santeuil*, and *Les Plaisirs et les jours*), he has apparently not made a close connection between inversion and memory's remarkable capacity of regaining sensations by way of signs. Nor has he connected this remarkable aspect of memory with the shock inflicted by his mother's loss – with her death or her being put to death. The full intensity of his remorse has to wait for its expression until 1921, the publication of *Sodom and Gomorrah*. And yet his sense of guilt echoes throughout his private correspondence, and gives itself away in the initial volumes through a number of characters who find their place there, such as Mlle Vinteuil, before finally, and with a minimal attempt at disguise, installing the figure of the mother at the heart of all the 'intermittencies of the heart'. The mother is at the heart of a primal sado-masochism.

Love is anguish, anguish is the putting to death – of whom?

The well-known scene of the kiss withheld at the little boy's bedtime, already told in *Jean Santeuil* and repeated in *Swann's Way*, has given generations of readers the image of a mother who is loved voraciously and selfishly. This was a love which involved, right from the start, a struggle for power, a mingling of violence and passivity, of desire and contrition. For the moment she yielded, the moment the kiss was granted, the narrator's anticipated triumph turned to bitter regret, and suffering began to colour his pleasure in a foretaste of sado-masochism.[6]

As early as 1896, in *Les Plaisirs et les jours*, Proust had written the 'Confession of a young girl' whose 'voluptuous and blameworthy' eroticism, though remaining heterosexual, is the cause of her mother's death.[7] Sex is shown to be intrinsically sadistic, as cruel to the lovers themselves as it is to their mothers. Proust writes: 'Now I was beginning to realize in a confused way that every act which is both voluptuous and blameworthy involves in equal measure the ferocity of the body taking its pleasure, and the tears and martyrdom of our good intentions and our guardian angels.'[8] It is through witnessing an erotic scene that the mother of the young girl who speaks these words is struck with apoplexy and dies.

After the death of Proust's own mother, we find him on 4 December 1905 at the clinic of Dr Sollier, a specialist in mental and nervous diseases, with the firm intention of proving that medicine can do nothing in his particular case. He succeeds, and leaves the establishment after six weeks. Social and literary life, so it would appear, are better at turning the activity of mourning into literature. Proust sets up house at 102 Boulevard Haussmann, and the architect Louis Parent lines his bedroom walls with cork in 1909: his cell is ready at just the same time as his plan for the work which will necessitate breaking open this shell, and dominating himself by a massive act of willpower which will be as delightful to experience as it is relentless in its effect on others.

From 1905 to 1909, Proust publishes little. Yet one thing that takes our attention is the article appearing in *Le Figaro* of 1 February 1907 under the title 'Filial Sentiments of a Parricide'. Proust's notice had been drawn, shortly after his mother's death, to an incident in which a person of his acquaintance, Henri Van Blarenberghe, had killed his mother and then committed suicide. Proust interpreted this as the aggressiveness of an Oedipus or an Orestes, known in cruel detail from the Greek texts. The further commentary which he added from Shakespeare and Dostoevsky was hardly less cruel. Obviously the murdering son is a criminal, but Proust the writer seems to be on the point of absolving him when he exclaims: 'what was the religious atmosphere of moral beauty in which this explosion of madness and slaughter took place?' (CSB, 157). He seems tempted to include himself in this crime: 'What have you made of me?' he asks. 'What have you made of me?':

If we put our minds to it, there would perhaps be not one truly loving mother who was not able, on her last day, and often long before, to address this reproach to her son. Basically, as we grow old, we all kill those who love us by the preoccupation we cause in them, by that very restless tenderness which we breathe in and put ceaselessly on its guard. (CSB, 158–9)

In January 1908 Proust writes 'Robert and the Kid. Mother leaves on a journey', a text which is now lost. The metamorphosis is under way: in 1909, the plan for a book on Sainte-Beuve turns into a genuine novel. Writing *Against Sainte-Beuve*, Proust the essayist explains that it is not through biography that the work of authors can be explained; talent has its own rationale, which society cannot comprehend. Here it is not just a matter of doing away with biography but, more exactly, of going into mourning for it. Proust takes up the project of *Jean Santeuil* again and transposes it. He searches for lost time in the innermost signs of his experience, infusing the singularity of his own grief into the universal pattern of an intelligence which is accessible to all. He starts working hard; his reclusiveness increasingly takes him over. In 1912 the first part of *A la recherche* reaches its completed form. In 1913 *Swann's Way* is published.

At this stage, Céleste Albaret enters Proust's service and makes it possible for him to live in perfect retirement in spite of his very demanding social life: through this means, and both through and in spite of his asthma, Proust is able to achieve the extraordinary ascetic life which will enable him to trace, with a sick but authoritative hand, the word END at the conclusion of *Time Regained*.

The governess: a daughter and a mother

Straight away, the writer recognizes in his female servant the marks of motherly love: that of a daughter for her mother, and that of a mother for her daughter. 'Your young wife is bored without her mother, Albaret, that's all,' he says to his chauffeur, Céleste's husband, before taking her into his service.[9] Céleste describes herself, in the year 1913, as 'a child in spite of my 22 years [Proust was 32] above all because I had only just left my mother's tender care behind'.[10] Master and servant will combine together in joint homage to the maternal. 'I was very fond of Papa. But Mama, the day she died, took her little Marcel with her.'[11] 'The nice thing about him was that I sometimes felt like his mother, and at others like his child.'[12] 'Everything affecting mothers and their experiences reminded him of his own and affected him deeply.'[13] 'It was particularly about my mother that he used to ask me questions. He would say to me: "It is easy to see that your father was a good man. But even with the best of men, the bread of human kindness will never be what it can be with a woman; there is always an outer shell of roughness. A man can never be the soul of kindness, as your mother seems to have been." '14

This kindness was, however, in Céleste's estimation, what Proust had managed to realize in himself, making him behave in such a way that the housekeeper, who was herself always taking infinite pains to seek out for him sole, smelts, gudgeons and fumigating powder, felt herself to be under the maternal care of her master. 'Monsieur, I find my mother again in you.' And, as Proust explained to Céleste: 'The thing is, you were made for devotion like your mother, even if you knew nothing about it. Otherwise, you would not be here.'15

Never can two beings more disparate in their background and level of education have been thus brought together in their devotion to the 'good mother', who would fill them both, alternately, with the sublimated love that binds a child to its mother, and no doubt the writer to his work. The mother who brings desire and guilt is dead; there remains complicity and the benefit of mutual silence. Céleste becomes the living relay between the female body and the book, between the turbulence of eroticism and the definitive form of the signed text. With a charming *naïveté*, she admits to having taken the place of a possible Albertine, an ideal Albertine, who, in her maternal devotion to the most motherly of sons, allows him not to marry her but to absorb her into a book:

Not only did I live at his rhythm, but you could say that, twenty-four hours out of twenty-four, and seven days out of seven, I lived exclusively for him. I have nothing to do with the person in his books whom he called 'The Captive', and yet I really deserved the title.16

Proust leans on her, and against her, he watches her but does not see her, he speaks to her and his words rebound off her. This is not a dialogue, she simply activates the monologue, by relaying and starting it up again; he forgets her, he gathers her up, she vanishes, as, moreover, does he. There is no longer any 'self', just the I that speaks across her.

So Céleste and the cork lining of his apartment on the Boulevard Haussmann, guarantee the air-tightness of the protected environment in which involuntary memory remakes and unmakes its tentacular sentences, on the look-out for sounds, colours and flavours; and at the same time there is another stage on which the great world keeps up its pretence, sex spends its fury and, soon enough, the war will arrive to turn existing hierarchies upside down. A number of authors talk of Proust at this period as being curious to witness scenes of debauchery. Maurice Sachs mentions rats pierced with hat-pins; M. Jouhandeau the photos of Proust's mother which were profaned in front of gigolos, the family furniture which was carried to the Le Cuziat brothel, the masturbation sessions where the voyeur hid in bed, with a naked young man before him, responding only to the pleasure of seeing rats devour one another.[17] This entire world expands and stages in the most grotesque fashion the sado-masochism which the narrator of *A la recherche* re-creates in a muted, psychological colouring; it unfolds as a kind of antithesis which works in conjunction with the writing laboratory where Céleste is the vestal virgin. The physical stimulus of debauchery serves to excite the senses and the emotions, with their blend of exaltation and abasement. No one can state categorically, however, that the pleasure of the childhood memory which has been given a name – and that of the scraps of paper which are mounting up all the time in his manuscript – is not as great as, or even greater than, the sexual intoxication.

Sublimation / profanation

So the mother is dead, I have killed her, my grief turns to remorse, I speak of it before another, I speak to myself, *I* speak – and all is regained, eternity.

The way has been prepared for the profanation which becomes possible after two or three years of mourning, in the course of which the loved person has become blurred in the memory, with no lessening in the mean time of the ambivalence of a guilt-ridden love.

As early as 1908, in Notebook 1, the hero dreams that his grandmother is dead, but the actual episode, 'Death of my grandmother', is forecast only in the plan of the 1912 version of the novel. The theme of inversion becomes steadily more important from 1908 onwards; sketches for the character of Charlus help to achieve the separation between essay and novel in the writing of *Against Sainte-Beuve*, and at the same time this project takes second place to the strictly narrative undertaking which is to be *A la recherche*. Meanwhile, over the years 1908 to 1912, the Proustian idea of profaning the mother takes root: Notebook 1 refers to 'the mother's face in a debauched grandson'.[18] Profanation is seen as a condition of sublimation. In *Against Sainte-Beuve* we read: 'The face of a son who lives on, like a monstrance in which a sublime mother, now dead, placed all her faith, is like the profanation of a sacred memory.' In *Sodom and Gomorrah*, finally, there is this late addition to the text:

Moreover, was it possible to separate M. de Charlus's appearance completely from the fact that, as sons do not always bear a likeness to their fathers, even when they are not inverts and go after women, they consummate in their faces the profanation of their mothers? But let us leave at this point what would be worth a chapter on its own: 'profanation of the mother'. (III. 300)

The interweaving of the two themes – inversion on the one hand, and on the other ambivalence towards the mother resulting in profanation – comes clearly into view, for example in Notebook 47, which opens with 'M. Charlus and the Verdurins' and continues with the grandmother's illness. When he later draws the connection between the death of his grandmother and that of Albertine, the narrator feels himself to be 'soiled with a double assassination'; at least, as Georges Bataille has pointed out, he believes himself to be responsible for profaning his mother in just the same way as Mlle Vinteuil profaned the memory of her father: the young girl makes him die of sorrow, and just a few days later, while still in mourning, enjoys the embraces of a lesbian lover who spits on the dead man's photograph. The sufferings of Vinteuil, who is shocked by his daughter's sexuality, are presented to us in place of the description which the reader expects, but will never receive, of the sorrows experienced by the narrator's mother in the face of Albertine (or Albert) coming on the scene:

he saw himself and his daughter in the lowest depths, and his manners had of late been tinged with that humility, that respect for persons who ranked above him and to whom he now looked up . . . that tendency to search for some means of rising again to their level, which is an almost mechanical result of any human downfall. (1. 162)

In a similar way, however, the narrator's mother is said to be so aware of the sufferings of the old piano teacher that she seems to share them from the inside.

At times when pleasure overtakes him, the narrator feels that he 'makes his mother's soul weep'. Like Mlle Vinteuil, who is an artist in sadism, he even comes to believe that sensual pleasure is a form of wickedness in which he can engulf himself and bury his ideal. For the ideal, which is uncompromisingly maternal, is so scrupulous and coercive that, to escape from it, you have to profane it, and drag it down into the bestial world of pleasure. The complicity which Proust discovers between the requirements of an ideal tenderness and the depths of transgression which it imposes is what renders the pervert miserable and, by the same token, deserving of love. Georges Bataille recognizes the kinship with his own inner experience of the ecstasies of sin and profanation when he writes: 'This wish for limitless horror reveals itself in the end for what it is: the true measure of love.'[19]

As for Albertine, she appears in the novel only around 1913, almost exactly at the same time as Céleste is becoming established in the apartment on the Boulevard Haussmann. Thanks to these two, Albertine and Céleste, the inversion can be concealed – there is a woman to embody the passion of the narrator, transposing the feeling that Proust reserves for men – and the element of profanation gets toned down. Certainly the narrator's mother would have no time for Albertine – but surely it is inflicting on her no more than a polite and conventional form of cruelty that he should desire a woman in this completely natural way?

Everything conspires in favour of sublimation: the grievous experience of passion, which has been filtered through mourning and trapped by the cork-lined wall of the motherly Céleste, can now break out in joy:

Ideas come to us as the successors to griefs, and griefs, at the moment when they change into ideas, lose some part of their power to injure our heart; the transformation itself, even, for an instant, releases suddenly a little joy. (III.944)

The imagination, the reflective faculty may be admirable machines in themselves but they may also be inert. Suffering sets them in motion. And then at least the woman who poses for us as grief favours us with an abundance of sittings, in that studio which we enter only in these periods and which lies deep within us. (III.946)

Accident, ageing and war

In the last volume of *A la recherche*, we are presented with three different forms of death: Albertine's accident, the ageing of the main characters, and the upheaval caused in society by the First World War. Without pausing to look at the aspects of this concern in detail, we can certainly show how Proust turns didactic, and outlines the way in which linear time can be transformed into the timelessness of literature. We can follow in *Time Regained* the successive stages through which he imposes his logic upon the innumerable flashbacks, condensations, plots and digressions which made up the earlier volumes of *A la recherche*.

As it restores my various, different, relationships with people and things, my memory fastens upon particular 'sites' and 'places'. But, incapable of placing them in succession to one another, it sets up 'revolutions' around me as it does around them. In order to take account of this assembly of 'revolutions', the book would have to use *'not the two-dimensional psychology* which we normally use but a quite different sort of *three-dimensional psychology'* (III.1087).

So through juxtaposing the 'opposing facets' – as in the face of Mlle de Saint-Loup, the 'masterpiece' which combines the features of a Swann and a Guermantes, an Odette and a Gilberte – Proust discovers what will be (and indeed already has been) the 'spur' of the book. This will impel the narrator (it already has impelled him) to create a world as vast as a *cathedral*, or on a more modest scale to arrange the pieces of material among themselves as if making a *dress* (III.1090).

The process of reasoning now reaches its fulfilment, and the

[23]

formula of *A la recherche*, its alchemical key, is waiting to be spoken. What the narrator calls an 'enhanced' place in time – perceived by the senses, inaccessible no doubt but, as the prepositional form 'à la' indicates, always beckoning to us, remaining open and disposable as the self revolves around it – is the notion of *embodied time*. The time in which all of our sensations are reflected upon, as they tie the knot between subjectivity and the external world and recover once again the sounds that lie beneath the masks of appearance:

This notion of *Time embodied*, of years past but not separated from us, it was now my intention to emphasize as strongly as possible in my work. And at this very moment, in the house of the Prince de Guermantes, as though to strengthen me in my resolve, the noise of my parents' footsteps as they accompanied M. Swann to the door and the peal – resilient, ferruginous, interminable, fresh and shrill – of the bell on the garden gate which informed me that at last he had gone and that Mamma would presently come upstairs, these sounds rang again in my ears, yes, unmistakably I heard these very sounds, situated though they were in a remote past. And as I cast my mind over all the events which were ranged in an unbroken series between the moment of my childhood when I had first heard its sound and the Guermantes party, I was terrified to think that it was indeed this same bell which rang within me and that nothing that I could do would alter its jangling notes. On the contrary, having forgotten the exact manner in which they faded away and wanting to re-learn this, to hear them properly again, I was obliged to block my ears to the conversations which were proceeding between the masked figures all round me . . . (III.1105)

Then, without warning, appearing like a confession a few lines before the word 'END' is inserted, there comes into play once again the notion of desire, and nothing less than the desire to destroy, on the extreme boundaries of cruelty. There is the sense of something coming into view and then being annihilated, of love and hate: the avowal that desire is in essence a perverse desire is what makes time regained come full circle:

And it is because they contain thus within themselves the hours of the past that human bodies have the power to hurt so terribly those who love them, because they contain the memories of so many *joys* and *desires* already effaced for them, but still *cruel* for the lover who contemplates and prolongs in the dimension of Time the beloved body of which he is jealous, so jealous that he may even wish for its *destruction* . . . Albertine deep down, whom I saw sleeping and who was dead.[20] (III. 1106) [my italics]

And yet, after this avowal of cruelty, it is *formal language* that passes on the message of the perversity at the root of all desire: the 'monsters' which take up their places within us come to form a kind of *polytopia* – 'a place . . . prolonged past measure – for simultaneously, like giants plunged into the years, they touch epochs that are immensely far apart, separated by the slow accretion of many, many days – in the dimension of Time. The End.' (III. 1107)

The End. Over and beyond the time of jealousy, the time for the construction of the work now takes over, in so far as the book is itself the direct replacement for the loved person – could we therefore refer to this Proustian time (of cruelty, sensation and writing) as a temporality of concern? Heidegger's 'temporality of concern' incorporates several different stages: the temporality of disclosedness, the temporality of understanding, the temporality of state of mind and the temporality of falling.[21] Yet desire, in its cruelty, goes beyond the temporality of concern, and opens up a place in which signs can develop a spatial dimension by building up sensations. The writer is no philosopher: memory regained bears the imprint of colour, taste, touch and other forms of experience, whilst a distinctive type of writing which transgresses all bounds in its richness of metaphor and its embedding of clauses one within one another at the same time destroys and reconstructs the world. In the Proustian text the non-temporal nature of the unconscious (as Freud would have it) goes side by side with an overpowering awareness of Being. The psychic absorbs the cosmic and, beyond it, Being itself is diluted in style.

So imaginary experience is not unaware of the temporality of concern. But it goes beyond it, in a search for joy. Closer in this sense to Spinoza than to Heidegger, Proust's fiction reveals fundamental features of the human psyche. Personally, I enjoy this revelation; I hope that you do too.

II
IN SEARCH
OF MADELEINE

———————

'At the age when Names [offer] us
an image of the unknowable' (II. 4)

In my first lecture, I tried to demonstrate the Proustian text as *experience*: not merely as a stylistic structure but as subjective, unconscious, sensory experience. I will now illustrate this further through an analysis of the famous episode of the madeleine cake, which will take us outside the framework of textual analysis. Of course, I shall be using some devices of stylistic analysis, and I shall be referring to 'textual genetics' in my account of the manuscript versions. But my main attention will go to the sensory experience underlying the involuntary memory.

Flavoursome, incestuous, bland, indeterminate – diluted in the tea but coagulating the locations of Combray – the 'little madeleine' cake offers a flavour of Proust to those who have never read him. But take another point of view, and the madeleine is a cliché which gets in the way of the cathedral: it becomes fixed in a flat image, loses its friability, and extends a veil of *ennui* over those endless sentences swarming with scents, sounds, colours and forms, with delicacies for the taste and delights for the touch, all unceremoniously soaked up by this notorious madeleine. So what if we tried to acquire a taste for it once again? To wake up our mouths, tongues and palates; to revive our dreams and memories; to go in search of all the pages once set aside and forgotten, where there may perhaps lie slumbering equivalents for the madeleine –

doubles, echoes, metaphors of it – which will enhance or tone down its mysterious flavour, but at any rate give it a new lease of life?

The taste of childhood regained emanates from *A la recherche* as it ends and comes full circle. We think we are at the beginning, and yet the entire closed spiral made manifest by the last book has already been set into motion, magnetized, to go in search of a deeper level which is certainly that of childhood but, at the same time, absorbs the further destiny which has already come to its close. So the circles of metamorphosis work their magic. The child is an adult who recalls having loved with his mouth persons and places that his adult desires regard as merely anodyne.

This is a story with eight successive stages, which are encapsulated in the last few pages of Proust's *Overture* (I. 46–51). I shall go through them in turn.

Stage 1: just a 'luminous patch'

We start with a memory of frustration and grief – 'the bare minimum of scenery necessary to the drama of my undressing', 'as though there had been no time there but seven o'clock at night' (I. 47). The two floors are reduced to a 'sort of luminous patch', by the always untimely arrival of M. Swann ('the unwitting author of my sufferings'), a guest who will take the mother's attention. The 'residue' of Combray is dead to memory; it can be brought back again only through the use of voluntary memory, by the use of the 'intellect'; which is much as to say that this 'residue' is without meaning.

Rapidly forgotten, diluted in the cup of tea *à la madeleine*, this patch will none the less be revived in a dramatic fashion in *La Prisonnière (The Captive)*. Bergotte, the writer, rediscovers a 'little patch of yellow wall' (which he had forgotten about) in a painting by Vermeer, praised by a critic as being 'like some priceless specimen of Chinese art, of a beauty that was sufficient in itself' (III. 185). The 'aridity and pointlessness of art', not excluding his own, are starkly revealed to Bergotte as he stands before this masterpiece, which humiliates and bemuses him. ' "My last books are too dry, I ought to have gone over them with a few layers of colour, made my language precious in itself, like this little patch of yellow wall." ' Either because of the indigestion he has caught from eating under-cooked potatoes, or because of the renewed effect prompted by the 'little patch of yellow wall', Bergotte then collapses and dies.

The narrator of *A la recherche*, for his part, seems not to worry about the challenge of the other arts. Proust's sentences compete with painting and music on their own terms; and the sequel to this story has shocks in store for us that put the little patch in the shade. And yet the idea of death (of a dead past, except for the 'luminous patch, sharply defined against a vague and shadowy background') has already been raised, and here it associates the disappearance of the anti-Proust represented by the writer Bergotte with the impossibility of bringing a childhood memory to life again. It is to be precisely in the sequel to this episode that the death of the past will be repudiated, and the whole flavour of childhood encapsulated, with layer upon layer of sensations, in a little cake.

Stage 2: the metamorphosis of the dead

There is a belief that the souls of the dead become the captives of inferior beings, such as animals, plants and inanimate objects, and survive within them in a completely changed and unrecognizable form. Might it not be the same for our own past, suggests the narrator. Tentatively, the hope of breathing new life into it is broached. It may be hidden 'in some material object (in the sensation which that material object will give us)'. For us to come across it once again is just a matter of luck.

Stage 3: I have the luck to taste a madeleine

One winter's day, when the dispirited narrator is persuading himself yet again that 'nothing of Combray, save what was comprised in the theatre and drama of [his] going to bed there, had any existence for [him]', his mother offers him a cup of tea accompanied by 'one of those squat, plump little cakes called "petites madeleines", which look as though they had been moulded in the fluted valve of a scallop shell'. In its unusual, moulded form, a kind of mushroom born of a shell, the madeleine stands between the narrator and his mother in the same way as George Sand's *François le champi* had done a few pages before (I. 42). For the madeleine scene is a sequel to a story which has already begun – one in which, immediately before our episode, the reading of *François le champi* by the mother of the narrator (at this point, a pampered child) forms a bond in voice and sensation between the future novelist and his progenitor, with no Swann and no bedtime dramas to worry about, simply the two of them bathed in a luke-warm atmosphere which is not yet teatime but is redolent of a warm, wet kiss.

Having left behind the damp world of the mother's reading, we find it again in the underwater associations of the madeleines, their links with aquatic bivalves and shellfish. But why these madeleines, in the first place? And why do we have to start by writing the word with a capital letter?

The first version of the text (in Notebook 8 of the 1909 manuscript) merely refers to a dry 'rusk'.[1] The term 'madeleine' appears in Draft 14 – nine pages cut out of a notebook which have been paginated from 1 to 9 and are identified as 'the fair copy of a very densely worked out rough of *Notebook 25*'. Are these pages from an unidentified notebook also from 1909, like 'Notebook 25', or did Proust complete his fair copy at a later stage? Did he perhaps put the fair copy in the 1909 notebook because of the similarity of content rather than because both belonged to the same period of writing? We can leave the question open for the moment. It is important, since we have to examine the motives that led Proust to give the name 'madeleine' to the most significant confectionery in his book.

The original reference in the name dates back, of course, to the well-known female sinner of the Gospels, a woman from Magdala, hence Magdalena. However, the common name of 'madeleine' was applied in the seventeenth century to the fruits sold around the season of St Mary Magdalene – peaches, plums, apples and pears – and it continued its alimentary career in the nineteenth century by being used for cakes (according to the Bescherelle dictionary, this was a tribute to a cook called Madeleine Paulmier). Even now, this ancestry is evocative enough to explain its interest for the writer. But, given Proust's sustained attention to names ('Place-names: the name' is the title of the third section of *Swann's Way*), and the meticulous care that went into choosing the proper names of the characters in the novel, we might be justified in taking the inquiry further and asking what lurks behind the transformation of the prosaic biscuit into a name possessed by a female sinner, then by a saint, and finally by a common sweetmeat.

'A name: that very often is all that remains for us of a human being, not only when he is dead, but sometimes even in his life-time.' (III. 1012) Into the syllables of names there

[33]

gravitate sensations and pleasures which are capable of exciting our imagination and magnetizing our desires. The name of Parma is 'compact, smooth, purplish and sweet', because of its heavy syllable 'in which there is no air circulating and because of all the Stendhalian sweetness and reminiscence of violets which I have made it absorb'. Florence has an embalming effect, like the corolla of a flower, because of being called the city of lilies, and because of its cathedral, Santa Maria dei Fiori – Saint Mary of the Flowers. 'Balbec [is] of old Norman pottery, earthen-coloured.' Names cause the imagination to crystallize, they possess a magic within themselves. 'Sometimes, hidden in the heart of its name, the fairy is transformed to suit the life of our imagination, by which she lives . . . However, the fairy languishes if we come into contact with the real person to whom her name corresponds.' (II. 5)

So what fairy is hiding within the proper name of Madeleine, and, even more tucked away, within the common name for the confectionary?

Repeating the same sounds, using the identical syllables over again, gives us 'a sensation from a bygone year', and enables us to gauge 'the distance' between the dreaming states that have been marked, each in their turn, by these identical tones. So a noble name becomes like a balloon filled with oxygen; you have only to burst it and, by this act of mischief, which is quite childish, after all, you let out the air of Combray, the scent of the hawthorn blossom, the rain, the sunshine, and the sacristy . . . Childhood is indeed the 'age when Names [offer] us an image of the unknowable', which is let down by the reality of people and things but can happily be recovered by the memory beneath the sound that once entranced the child's ear (II. 4–6).

This is a type of reasoning which works for geographical

names, like Bayeux, Vitré, Coutances, Lannion, Quimperlé, Pontorson etc., as it does for the prestigious name of Guermantes. But will it perhaps work in other cases? The answer lies in using the same sounds once again, and in manipulating them even to the point of destroying, or bursting, the proper name so that it loses its uncommon nature, but at the same time releases, through the oxygen of memory, a plethora of sensations, impressions and delights, 'in which we suddenly feel the original entity quiver and resume its form, carve itself out of syllables now dead' (II. 6).

Stage 4: incest and silence – the disappearance of two women's names

Here the text is in need of an intertext. The narrator's grandmother – a great admirer of George Sand – had made him a present of Sand's 'four pastoral novels': *La Mare au diable*, *François le champi*, *La petite Fadette* and *Les Maîtres Sonneurs*. ' "My dear," she had said to Mamma, "I could not bring myself to give the child anything that was not well written." ' (I. 42) In this way, readings from George Sand come to form a special link between the son and his mother. In the earlier versions of the text, Proust speaks simply of 'a volume by George Sand', referring to *La Mare au diable*.[2] In Notebooks 8[3] and 10, however, two texts get mentioned, *La Mare au diable* and *François le champi*.[4] The mother is still shown as reading two of George Sand's texts up to the typewritten manuscript destined for *Le Figaro*, usually dated 1909,[5] in which Proust finally crosses out *La Mare au diable*. *François le champi* is left on its own in the bedtime episode which precedes that of the madeleine.

Less 'pastoral' than the other three novels, *François le champi* (1850) tells the story of a foundling child (*champi* is the term for 'foundling' in the Berry dialect) who is taken in by the miller's wife, Madeleine Blanchet, becomes the object of her unwitting love, and later, on his return to the village as an adult, her lover and husband, his adoptive mother having become a widow.

Proust was to be a severe critic of George Sand in his later writings,[6] but he nevertheless retained this central reference to *François le champi*, continuing to allow the reading of it a structural role in the scaffolding of *A la recherche*. Even in *Time Regained*, when the narrator is in the library of the Prince de Guermantes, it is this 'pastoral' volume that provokes the fourth of his reminiscences and leads to his aesthetic revelation. There is therefore good reason to think that, however much he may have disapproved of George Sand's style, it is precisely the theme of incest, the sinning mother, that secured and maintained Proust's interest in *François le champi*. The role of the miller's wife, Madeleine Blanchet, would be one of communicating, through her floury whiteness, the taste of the forbidden love that will find its way into the narrator's main aesthetic credo – a taste which has been metamorphosed into an apparently anodyne object: the little madeleine.

Yet in reading the various versions of the text, one is struck by two small facts which throw an interesting light on Proust and the genesis of his writing. The first has to do with the appearance, and later the disappearance, of Madeleine Blanchet's name in the text. In the first typewritten version, which has already been mentioned, after 'This predisposed me to imagine that *François le champi* contained something inexpressibly delicious', Proust writes:

The opening pages are very simple: Madeleine Blanchet, the miller's wife of Cormoner, discovers in her field a child who is playing in front of the fountain where she washes her linen. But the fact that this country woman, this small child, this fountain and this field formed part of a novel gave them an extraordinary attraction in my eyes. And then I felt that this meeting between the miller's wife and the child was *something* [added to the MS in Proust's hand] more than *what* [added to the MS in Proust's hand] it [crossed out] appeared to be, that it would later become important for the life of the characters, that it was not just a detached episode, but a beginning which reached towards an unknown future.[7]

This passage, which appears in Notebook 10 originally and as a fair copy in the typescript, is left out of the subsequent versions. Madeleine Blanchet is retained at the proof stage,[8] but she is omitted from the printed text based on the corrected proofs, as well as from the third stage of the proofs.[9] This devastating elimination took place within a month, and obviously there must have been an intermediate text, which is now missing, between the two manuscripts NA Fr. 16754 and 16755, in which Proust would have crossed out in his own hand the passage concerning Blanchet. We can only conclude that he had thought about the matter beforehand, and had already taken the decision in his mind to expel the miller's wife from the text, because she had no further role to play there. But why? Is it simply going too far to speak of an incestuous mother before dealing with sweetmeats? Or did the peasant love story no longer seem quite up to the level of Proust's aesthetic and sensual ambitions, being 'as unwholesome as sweets and cakes'? What was the reason for Madeleine Blanchet's disappearance, and at what stage, precisely, did it take place?

Here we have a second fact to take into account in determining how this part of the novel came to take the form it did.

On 1 March 1896, the literary review *La Vie contemporaine* published under the signature of Marcel Proust a novella entitled *L'Indifférent*, which would remain unknown to the literary public until it was reissued in 1978 by Philip Kolb.[10] It is not irrelevant to mention how Kolb himself came upon this youthful text by Proust. In a letter of 1910 to his friend Robert de Flers, Proust inquires if he has in his possession a copy of *La Vie contemporaine*, because he has mislaid his own and needs one: 'I wrote a silly novella there, which I am now in need of, and you would do me a service if you could send me the number.'

What goes on, then, in this 'silly novella'?

A noble lady falls in love with a young man who shows nothing but indifference towards her. Increasingly attracted by this individual, whose surname features in a famous painting by Watteau, she ends by finding out that young Lepré's coldness is a cover for his passionate attachment to prostitutes: 'He loves the ignoble women who are found in the gutter and he loves them to distraction.'[11] The connection between this plot and the love life of Swann is a plausible one, and Kolb demonstrates it convincingly. Swann is indeed the lover of a tart, Odette de Crécy, whom he rescues from the street and prepares for a brilliant career; one that will be difficult at first, but in the end crowned with worldly success – all the more so after the death of her husband and the altered society that succeeds the war. Odette could be seen as an amalgam of the women loved by Lepré and the noble lady to whom he is entirely indifferent – a high and mighty aristocrat whose prototype may well have been the Comtesse Greffulhe: covered in flowers, 'without a single jewel, her corsage of yellow tulle covered with cattleyas, and she had also attached a few cattleyas to her dark coiffure'. These cattleyas later become the fetish-word of Odette and Swann, 'to do a cattleya' (meaning, 'to make love') being the most intimate term in their private language. An essential aspect of the heroine of *L'Indifférent* has therefore been incorporated in the character of Odette in inverted form: the irreproachable *grande dame*, at the very opposite end of the scale from the 'ignoble' creatures who stimulate Lepré to vice, lends her floral charm to Odette, a process of transference which ennobles the *demi-mondaine* and profanes the aristocrat. It is easy to understand that, in creating Swann and his love life, Proust needed to go back to the heroine of *L'Indifférent*, whom he had certainly not forgotten but wished to study again in detail.

Yet it happens that the commentators who see her living again in Odette have forgotten to mention the name of this high and mighty aristocrat. She is called Madeleine de Gouvres. Odette has robbed her of her cherished flower. But Madeleine de Gouvres retains her nobility and thoughtfulness, putting us in mind of an inaccessible presence which is familiar but forbidden, familial and lofty at the same time: the very image of a loved mother who is cut off from us by a patch of light and drama. This image of Madeleine de Gouvres will not go away. As with the superstition which the narrator mentions in Stage 2 of our episode, the souls of the dead can become the captives of 'inanimate objects' – in particular, perhaps, if the identical sonorities and timbres of the names pronounced in the course of repeated dreaming and feeling revive and reanimate the remote presence of the fairies and their abodes. Madeleine will easily succeed in ousting the unfortunate rusk and in granting her maternal flavour, which is at the same time blandly inaccessible and delightfully exciting, to a little madeleine which lurks tasteless in my mouth, but also has the power to arouse insatiable desire. So the narrator will easily rediscover the forbidden pleasure of the mother's kiss (whose melancholy charms he had just recounted when Swann's arrival obliged him as a dutiful son to give it up and go to bed), not in the mother's mouth, nor even in her voice as she reads *François le champi*, but in a stumpy, fat little mushroom, dunked in tea and named, inevitably, a madeleine.

You may be right in seeing my determination to resurrect Madeleine Blanchet and Madeleine de Gouvres in this famous piece of confectionary as the fantasy of a mischievous or well-informed reader. I persist in it because, for one thing, Proust is no stranger to this kind of ironic but also tender transposition, and, for another, because 'the madeleine episode' – framed as it is by the memory of the mother rejected because she does not offer herself, and by the story of Swann – serves as a special invitation to us to reinstate the oral link which holds the narrator to a woman he loves, who is yet capable of remaining indifferent to him.

So you refuse to offer yourself, Mother? What does it matter? In any case, that pleasure means nothing to me, or will soon mean nothing. I have others which are not necessarily 'ignoble', but subtle and indefinable, going far beyond *François le champi*, your readings and your kisses. A cup of tea will do, and another woman, a paternal aunt, Aunt Léonie, who is more distant and reassuring, standing in your place; she will not let your intrusive closeness work its effect and haunt my beverage like those Japanese paper flowers which recover their magical shapes once they have been dipped in water. No, all I can taste is an indifferent madeleine, the deferred recollection of another thing, of another woman, a woman you could have been or have been but are no longer. I can guarantee that Odette has usurped the desirable situation; all we have is the polite indifference of a cup of tea. And my imaginings, in secret.

So it can be claimed that Madeleine de Gouvres lives a double life from now on. She is a 'silly' spectre, all right, but she does not leave Proust's imaginary life indifferent, she is not like a mother who abandons you: she is a woman you drop (as Lepré does) because she is all too worthy and you prefer the unworthy ones. Who is it that makes this choice? Lepré? Swann obviously does, for he prefers Odette, but only when he has ennobled her, adjusting her in the light of elegance and artistic inspiration, grafting the cattleyas on to her. The narrator himself is not unacquainted with Swann's adventures: after Gilberte (Swann's daughter) his choice will settle upon the barely presentable Albertine, who is a long way from gaining the approval of his respectable mother. Desire debases its object in order to get to it more effectively. Proust himself will push this principle to its absolute limit by placing his family furniture and photographs on show in a brothel.

Yet this logic of profanation is supported by another one, which it needs to reinforce in order to do away with it conclusively. It is a question of holding on, at any price, to the pure and candid flavour – like an afternoon tea with cakes – of the sensations aroused by the mother's presence. Of divesting it of its female sexuality, of its female corporeality, leaving behind nothing but the tender, loving care. Mary Magdalene has to be made a saint, but in a different way from the Gospels: the arousing aspect of womanhood, of motherhood, sets into inaccessiblity in *L'Indifférent*; yet at the same time it is destined to recover a modest strength in this exquisite satisfaction, oral by origin, which completely satisfies the son's recollection by causing a gamut of sensations to cluster around the name of the cake as woman and bring the house of his birth to life again.

At the same period (1909–10) Proust invents a female character whom he will later abandon in favour of Albertine: this is Maria, a young girl who excites the narrator's interest but later disappoints him. Maria is obviously linked to Madeleine: the phrase Marie-Madeleine means a female 'sinner'. However, Proust's tentative Maria is no more than a mediating device to conceal and contain his passion for the chauffeur Agostinelli. Albertine will be the definitive character charged with this role.

Marie-Madeleine none the less makes her return as such when the writer turns his attention to *The Guermantes Way*, in connection with Robert de Saint-Loup and his love for Rachel. Whilst the narrator remains completely indifferent to the actress, Saint-Loup is bowled over by her; he commits 'the crowning folly of making an inaccessible idol of a whore' (II. 162). The ways of the lover and those who remain impervious can never come together: 'It was not "Rachel when from the Lord", who seemed to me of little significance, it was the power of the human imagination.' (II. 162) The narrator, for his part, can picture the nearby fruit trees as gods, just as in the Gospel Mary Magdalene mistook the man of passion for a simple, indifferent gardener.[12] She calls to mind the distinctly worldly error which led Madeleine, in *L'Indifférent*, to be oblivious of Lepré's passion – not to mention Lepré's own blindness which made him, since he did not love her, incapable of responding to Madeleine de Gouvres' beauty. However, in the Gospel Mary Magdalene's bemusement is only temporary. She soon guesses that Jesus is present, that he has revealed to her the passion of his own flesh in order to assuage her grief. In this way we could see the saint as a double for the narrator himself: he has none of the lover's imagination which brings Saint-Loup to adore the prostitute, but he is himself to experience the delusory enthusiasms of the lover's imagination with Albertine. Indeed, she is destined to exert an enigmatic charm on the young man which his friends fail to comprehend, and which is presented as the exact counterpart of Saint-Loup's infatuation with Rachel. Love alone has the capacity to create metaphors and infuse images with the experience of time, as it does objects and names. It is love that makes a rusk into a cascade of involuntary memories, sweetly redolent of the lost sensation that can be re-created.

Let us note finally, as a provisional conclusion to this metaphorical and metamorphic series of madeleines and Marie-Madeleines, that the Princesse de Guermantes – the proud, though not particularly 'dressy', and teutonically stuck-up cousin of the inaccessible Oriane – has the Christian name Marie. This is the Marie-Gilberte whom Proust dressed, in her aquarium-box at the Opéra, in the way that Mme Standish did in reality; though she may be strange and distant, she is perhaps not indifferent under the weight of her toilette (II. 36–7).

It is, however, the Duchesse de Guermantes who keeps alive in *A la recherche* the flame of aesthetic and aristocratic prestige that the Comtesse Greffulhe kindled in the young Marcel, and that Madeleine de Gouvres shared for a brief moment. Oriane embodies the narrator's admiration for womanhood at its most sublime, even though, after the war and the Dreyfus affair – which are, to put it mildly, no respecters of persons – she will eventually be subjected to the same kind of ridicule as Mme Verdurin.

For the moment, though, we have been looking at the madeleine and Madeleine: the woman and the sweetmeat, the mother and the sinner, the one tasty, the other indifferent. Metaphor and metonymy succeed in irradiating the text, bringing places and moments together under the auspices of desire and condensing their intermittent appearances into a pure form of oral sensuousness. This is the nodal point of childhood memory – the book, the voice and the taste come together in fusion; Aunt Léonie gives Mamma a hand in order that a loving body can emerge from the cup of tea.

That this has been there from childhood Madeleine de Gouvres demonstrates, in her own way, in 1896. The narrator must unconsciously have associated her with the ambiguities of his desires when he replaced the rusk with a madeleine in 1909. His re-reading in 1910 of his novella *L'Indifférent*, sent by Robert de Flers, must obviously have confirmed him in this choice: the fair copy on the unidentifiable sheets dates perhaps from this re-reading, and so from 1910. In any case, 'madeleine'/Madeleine was already inscribed in his memory and in the text: a crossroads of flavours, women, sin, indifference and more or less sacred books, which has not yet lost its power to make us dream also.

Stage 5: an exquisite pleasure without origin

Let us return to the story. Softened in the tea, the mouthful of cake touches the palate, and this contact – which is the most infantile and archaic that a living being can possibly experience with an object or a person, since food like air is the exquisite necessity which keeps us alive and curious about our fellows – sets off an 'extraordinary process in me'. To be honest, it is a pleasurable sensation. 'An exquisite pleasure had invaded my senses, something isolated, detached, with no suggestion of its origin.' (1.48)

The 'origin' remains behind in the salon, the 'origin' refuses to kiss or read, the 'origin' is a noble lady who believes her son to be indifferent without suspecting – though she may have had a presentiment of the fact – that indifference is fostered by vice. The origin has become infused in the madeleine, without anyone being the wiser.

To recollect through the senses is just the same as being in love. Together, in conjunction, these two activities form the essence of the narrator. And so his *selves* can be directly equated with his recollections of love, and thus of sensory experience, which place him right at the opposite side of the scale from the humdrum accidents of everyday reality:

And at once the vicissitudes of life had become *indifferent* to me . . . this new sensation having had on me the effect which love has of filling me with a precious *essence*; or rather this essence was not in me, it *was* me. I had ceased now to feel mediocre, contingent, mortal. (1.48) [my italics]

This recollection, which partakes at the same time of love and of sensation, can be seen from now on as the vanquishing of a depressive stage, which yet remains enigmatic. 'Whence could it have come to me, this all-powerful joy?'

Proust raises the issue, even in these opening pages, of the naturalness of sensation. Since taste is a taste for tea and cakes, it is unquestionably rooted in the things of this world. Taste is of the world in just the same way as the experience which restores both taste and all the other forms of sensation. And yet at the same time the narrator is convinced that his experience has 'infinitely transcended' taste and sensation: it 'could not, indeed, be of the same nature'. Right from the start, in fact, this joy born of experience is a *meaningful* one: 'What did it mean?' asks the narrator.

The second mouthful produces nothing more than was in the first; the third is even less strong. *Sensation* as such is ebbing away: 'the potion is losing its magic. It is plain that the truth I am seeking lies not in the cup but in myself.' (1.48)

It remains only for the narrator to abandon the cup and address himself to the *mind*. The mind however is in a state of feeling 'overtaken', for it is not just a matter of searching to locate an experience which was formerly laid down there, in the same form, but of *creating* experience. 'Seek? More than that: create. It is face to face with something which does not yet exist, to which it alone can give reality and substance, which it alone can bring into the light of day.' (I.49)

Stage 6: desire and the visible

'I do not know yet what it is, but I can feel it mounting slowly.'

'The proof of this happiness' is an imponderable which escapes all categories of logic. The narrator will make an effort none the less to clarify the experience that he feels. And how? By, first of all, insulating himself from all his present sensations, especially those of hearing: he will stop his ears, and concentrate hard. But no, that is too rigorous and tiring. A better idea would be to cultivate a state of 'distraction': to 'clear an empty space'. So the still recent sensation of taste combines with what we must really call desire, as a lively, erotic impulse makes itself felt: 'I feel something start within me, something that leaves its resting-place and attempts to rise, something that has been embedded like an anchor at a great depth . . . I can feel it mounting slowly.' (I.49) Distance and resistance are overcome. And what is found?

An image. Taste has become a representation, it has changed into an 'elusive whirling medley of stirred-up colours'. Here indeed we have a 'form' in gestation which remains 'confused' and is incapable of 'translating' clearly its 'inseparable paramour', which is the taste.

It is a wonderful moment when the image mounts under the impulsion of desire. A moment to repeat, but then to leave behind: a moment which is disturbing, because of the 'difficult task' with which it confronts the narrator. We can note in passing how sensation and representation inevitably drift apart at the very moment when the experience of taste, as an immediate perceptual experience, is transcended by the concern to illuminate its meaning. *Taste* and *vision* are still inseparable paramours but they have come unstuck: this is the fundamental lack of fit between what is *perceived* and what is *signified*, and this the work is called upon to resolve – except that there is a cowardice, stemming from boredom and desire, which always succeeds in deterring the narrator from his task.

Stage 7: a substitution quietens the effervescence – Aunt Léonie in place of Mamma

'And suddenly' memory offers a substitution which will finally provide a stable *image* for the inconclusive effervescence of the narrator's identity and the gap between what is perceived and what is signified. For Mamma's madeleine is substituted the madeleine of Léonie, the father's sister around whom Proust arranges his memories of his paternal family, the Amiot of Illiers. There is a metonymic shift from mother to aunt, from present to past sensation. The flavour of the past, still slumbering in the depths of the memory, which had been thought, quite wrongly, to have disappeared, comes back again to endow with image and body the narrator's mounting sense of vertigo. Take note of the process: actual experience (the mother's madeleine) is imbued with a disabling intensity and gives rise to states of emptiness and confusion which would be ungovernable, if the narrator were not able to stabilize his pleasure through a displacement. The distance in time and space (Sunday before mass, with his aunt) affords a perception and an image which are analogous to what is experienced now, and without them the present experience would fall to pieces. This process of metonymic

[47]

transfer which opens up the domain of the past is the construction of a metaphor: Proust's madeleine is thus the condensation which embraces two moments in time and two different spaces within the 'vast structure of recollection' (1.51).

Stage 8: memory is a cascade of spatial metaphors

This point of equilibrium generates a chain of memories which is at the same time a cascade of spatial metaphors. The pleasure of taste is given full rein in the happy atmosphere of the dwellings of his childhood: the old grey house, the town square, the country roads in the vicinity, the flowers in the garden, Swann's park, the water-lilies on the Vivonne, the good folk of the village and the church of Combray. The modest 'patch of luminous wall' is forgotten, swept out of the way by the proliferation of cherished spaces. All becomes 'solid and recognizable', since an interval has been inserted between, on the one hand, the oral collapse in the mother's proximity which stirs up desires founded upon the proffered readings and the often withheld kisses, and, on the other hand, the stability of Aunt Léonie, who is set at a safe distance; it is her sickly, bourgeois and already a little ridiculous presence that will provide the focus for the observation of Combray.

There is one final metonymy of the madeleine: that of the magic Japanese scraps of paper which take on their form once they have been steeped in bowls filled with water. It is the definitive stabilization of the loss and transference of meaning and representation whose story is recounted to us in the episode of the madeleine.

Aunt Léonie after Mamma: Japan after Aunt Léonie: we are at the very antipodes of the place of birth. As if it were necessary to set up a maximum distance, a foreign country, to enable us to *see*, again to the maximum extent, how evanescent is the object of desire which the little madeleine offers to be *sensed*. Both elsewhere *and* here at hand, past *and* also present, a sensation *and* an image at the same time, just as it is both a name *and* a meaning – our madeleine is kneaded out of all of these and excites a taste for one as much as for the other. Mamma was a starting mechanism, and she is from now on a source of indifference to us, as is Madeleine de Gouvres. Now we are inside the imaginary world of the madeleines. And are we now indifferent to this, in turn? No. But it is a secret, and Proust's whole novel will be a search for the sweet as well as the ignoble aspects of this central erotic secret.

III
APOLOGIA
FOR METAPHOR

I

'to draw forth from the shadow
what I had merely felt'*

For Proust, sensation – made up of tension, contradiction, always at a crossroads – is at one and the same time 'imagination' and 'the actual shock to my senses', 'representation' and 'the essence of things', past and present; by virtue of the fact that it brings these opposites into conjunction, sensation is 'a fragment of time in the pure state' (III.905). Neither a reality nor mere solipsism, it exists at the interface of the world and the self. Proust is endeavouring to capture in language and communicate to us an element of his very own, what he calls 'being': the 'being' that had been 'reborn in me' but that takes its nourishment from 'the essence of things' where it 'finds its substance and its delight'. Perception of present reality is a disappointment, and only the imagination can provide lasting enjoyment, in its quest for what is absent ('reality had disappointed me because at the instant when my senses perceived it my imagination, which was the only organ that I possessed for the enjoyment of beauty, could not apply itself to it, in virtue of that ineluctable law which ordains that we can only imagine what is absent' (III.905)). But experience will in fact suspend the effects of this 'harsh law': imagination will apprehend a sound, in the past, at the very moment when the senses are being shocked by the same sound in the here and now. From this basis, Proust's 'being' can be reborn; it can become actual, present and real, with such a 'sudden shudder

* III.912   [53]

of happiness' that the 'true self' which had been thought dead will awaken emancipated from the régime of time. '[One] can understand that the word "death" should have no meaning for him; situated outside time, why should he fear the future?' (III.906)

Let us emphasize this two-faced 'being' which Proust seeks to name in his writing. Since it is infiltrated from the start by representation – that is to say, by a legacy of representations from the past – perception is always in a state of being stretched between the *world of the present* and the *historical self*; that is why it is bound to be 'subjective and incommunicable'. So a 'certain *name* read in a book some time in the past' contains not only ideas but, mixed in with its syllables, the sunny or windy weather of the time of our reading. However anchored it may be in 'what goes on around us', perception is no less rooted in 'the person that we were then'. Hence there results for Proust a kind of synonymous connection between 'sensibility' and 'thought': 'it remains also faithfully united to what we ourselves then were and thereafter it can be handled only by the *sensibility*, the personality that was then ours' (III.921).

When he turns his attention to this interface, Proust emphasizes one or other aspect of it in turn. Beneath 'signs', beneath 'the image', the narrator 'feels' something irreducible:

already at Combray I used to fix before my mind for its attention some *image* which had compelled me to look at it, a cloud, a triangle, a church spire, a flower, a stone, because I had the *feeling* that perhaps beneath these signs there lay something of a quite different kind. (III.912)

What would this be? The subject of feeling turns himself into a thinker (and some have gone so far as to see him as a Platonist[1]):

. . . something of a quite different kind which I must try to discover, some *thought* which they translated after the fashion of those *hieroglyphic* characters which at first one might suppose to represent only material objects. (III.912)

The interface brings together three elements: the *felt*, the *thought*, and the *impression* (which is also called 'hieroglyphic character' or 'cipher'). Intelligence which goes 'less deep' than the 'life' which affects us 'through our senses' is none the less capable of 'extracting its spiritual meaning'. Confronted with these closely related aspects, the writer will have the task of 'interpreting the given sensations as signs of so many laws and ideas'. In his double role as one who senses and one who meditates, he will think through his work, aiming 'to draw forth from the shadow — what I had merely felt, by trying to convert it into its spiritual equivalent' (III.912).

Between the 'shadow' of what is felt and its 'spiritual equivalent', Proust's novel imprints the network of its metaphors, its sentences and its mode of narration. The 'shadow' deepens at the same time as the 'equivalent' becomes more and more diffused. But is it ever a matter of one of them being sacrificed to the other?

2

Omnipresent analogy

Doublet and transsubstantiation

In line with these remarks, we must take into account that the minimal unit in the Proustian text is not the word-sign but a doublet: sensation and idea, perception represented or image made incarnate. The formal status of the signifier — so prized by the technicians of language — and the materiality, in linguistic terms, of the work of art are not so much rejected by Proust (though his argument with what he judges to be the 'obscure' formalism of Mallarmé lends support to this hypothesis) as they are spontaneously deduced from, and logically consequent upon, the subjective assertion which is Proust's own experience at the *crossroads* between the felt world of the present and the world of the self which belongs to the past. As we have argued already, Proust savours his *sensations* for their provision of the *essence* of things, so long as they link up with the conflicting desires of his own *personal history*: he leads the life of one of those 'transformed intelligences which has become embodied in matter . . . This transformation of energy in which the thinker disappears and things are laid out in front of us must surely be seen as the writer's first move in achieving a style?' (CSB, 612)

Proust once remarked to André Maurois: 'My work is not microscopic, it is telescopic.'[2] And it is worth making the hypothesis that this 'telescoping' has its psychological point of departure in an original state of *disappointment*, which has been powerfully overcome by the *hallucinatory capacity* to reproduce the desired but lost impressions within the imagination. 'Impressions such as those to which I wished to give permanence could not but vanish at the touch of a direct enjoyment which had been powerless to engender them.' (III.911)

Already present in the madeleine episode, the initially acute awareness of a separation between what is *felt* and what is *represented* becomes more marked as the plot progresses; as journeys, love affairs and finally the whole Faubourg Saint-Germain fail to please, the state of disappointment becomes a kind of *empty centre* around which what is felt and what is said continue to gravitate: this is our 'powerlessness to realize ourselves in material enjoyment or in effective action' (III.911). So it is only through *reproducing* them, through a movement that is indeed 'telescopic', or more precisely metaphorico-metonymic, involving displacement and condensation – from Mamma to Aunt Léonie in the case of the madeleine – that true sensory experience will be produced. Sensation must be recovered in the same way as time: it arrives after the event, in the form of words, and contrary to expectation, with old sensations being renewed in the here and now, and thus re-created: 'For I should have to execute the successive parts of my work in a succession of different materials . . . [in] a new and distinct material, of a transparency and a sonority that were special, compact, cool after warmth, rose-pink.' (III.903–4) Produced by the assemblage of two words (which may be a perception soldered to an idea, or two perceptions and two ideas, or two representations with 'common essences'), this 'new material' is none other than the *fusion of analogy*, the very stuff of metaphor. In a letter to Léon Daudet dated 27 November 1913, quoted by Gérard Genette, Proust raises the prospect of a way of writing 'in

[57]

which the supreme miracle would be accomplished, the transsubstantiation of the irrational qualities of matter and life into human words'.[3] This way of writing is his own: for those who are willing to pay attention to its double lining of sensation, metaphor achieves the feat of transsubstantiation dreamed of by the novelist.

'As long as there is none of that, there is nothing'

The operation which Proust refers to as 'analogy' or 'metaphor' has no connection with the same term as used by formalist rhetoric to designate the replacement of a well-worn – or abstract – term by another which is unusual or strange.[4] It is much more like the reciprocal relationship, one of contradiction maintained between the two terms, which more recent authors have tried to reinstate in maintaining the ambivalence of metaphorical expression.[5] If we appreciate the way in which the double nature of signs can be interiorized within the impressions of memory, we can understand better how intense is the form of condensation that Proust believes to be the *sine qua non* of literature:

... truth will be attained by [the writer] only when he takes two different objects, states the connection between them – a connection analogous in the world of art to the unique connection which in the world of science is provided by the law of causality – and encloses them in the necessary links of a well-wrought style; truth – and life too – can be attained by us only when, by comparing a quality common to two sensations, we succeed in extracting their common essence and in reuniting them to each other, liberated from the contingencies of time, within a metaphor. (III. 924–5)

A representation, for instance a seascape by Elstir, can work only as a *metamorphosis*: not just a simple name but, by virtue of the substitution of one name for another, the metaphor incarnate. The narrator observes that:

the charm of each of [the seascapes] lay in a sort of metamorphosis of the objects represented, analogous to what in poetry we call metaphor, and that, if God the Father had created things by naming them, it was by taking away their names or giving them other names that Elstir created them anew. The names which designate things correspond invariably to an intellectual notion, alien to our true impressions, and compelling us to eliminate from them everything that is not in keeping with that notion. (I. 893)

We have already noted that Proust establishes an equivalence between the imagination of the artist and the creativity of 'life' and 'nature': metaphor, in its turn, is just a way of becoming part of the continual weaving of connections that takes place at the heart of living, in the creative reality. Let us take note of two other features of this operation, without which (as Proust puts it) 'there is nothing'.

The 'connection' brings together different objects by virtue of their resemblances, as detected by the narrator. He superimposes, overprints one upon another, squeezing out the differences; in place of discrete units, he establishes 'links'. As a continuous linking together of circular elements, analogy has the effect of opening up the surface of signs in the direction of depth; as a creator of figures, the exponent of metaphor is like a geometrician, but in a more essential way he is an X-ray operator and surgeon. How does he work? How are the superimpositions effected? And what are the depths that they open up?

Metamorphic adventures of the Vinteuil 'little phrase'

The 'little phrase of Vinteuil', which Swann hears again at Mme Verdurin's house 'after having heard it the previous year', awakens a series of auditory sensations. With memory preparing the way, the 'little phrase' is from the start endowed with a power of recollection which anticipates the actual process of perception and gives rise to a whole range of pleasures which are expressed in a series of metaphors (I. 227–31).

Let us explore this series of metaphors a little further. The 'little phrase' is first of all, in the violin, 'slender but robust, compact and commanding' and at the same time, in 'the mass of the piano part', a 'liquid rippling of sound', 'deep blue tumult of the sea'. At the moment which follows the performance, it is 'as the fragrance of certain roses, wafted upon the moist air of the evening', 'confused', '*sine materia*'. Yet immediately afterwards, Swann rediscovers its 'extent, its symmetrical arrangements, its notation . . . design, architecture, thought'. A further connection is added on to this chain of 'links': when Swann returns home, he experiences the 'little phrase' as 'a woman he has seen for a moment passing by'. A new analogy occurs to him: the 'little phrase' opens up a possibility of 'rejuvenation', and, far from restricting himself to a mere logical excursus over the keyboard of his five senses, Swann literally feels himself to be rejuvenated. Metaphor has now become metamorphosis, a physical reality. The 'ramifications of [the little phrase's] fragrance' leave on Swann's features 'the reflection of its smile'. Finally he finds out the 'name' of his 'unknown woman' or 'phrase': it is the Andante from Vinteuil's Sonata for Piano and Violin. But, over and beyond the name expressed in technical language (without any concern for analogy), the succession of these metaphors and metamorphoses is enough for Swann to fall in love with this piece of music, for it to become the 'national anthem' of Odette and himself, for the aesthete to make the decision to marry Odette while loving in her not so much the woman, whom he no longer desires, as the work of art – Botticelli's *Zipporah* – and, above all, the 'little phrase' for which the young woman has henceforth become the metaphor or, more exactly, the metamorphosis. We can recall that the 'little phrase' was, for a moment, analogous to a person; in the last analysis, and by an inverted logic, Odette's person has become analogous to the 'little phrase'. The series of metaphors moves in the other direction: music is both woman and rejuvenation; woman will be a rejuvenating wife only to the extent that she is confused with music. The imagination of the aesthete and lover is required for this 'reciprocal metaphor'[6] to be fully forged, but this is possible only in so far as there has been a coincidence between the *analogy* (loving music, loving a woman) and the *contiguity* (Odette's presence at Swann's side while they listen to the 'little phrase' in the Verdurin salon).

Proust seems to be drawn to metaphors that are reversible in this way, and that enable him to establish a contiguity between analogies. (In just the same way, he uses expressions like 'impalpable water' and 'insoluble glass' (I. 184), with the contiguous substances exchanging their predicates.[7]) He calls these effects 'alliterations', thus choosing to create yet another analogy, drawn from the stock of rhetorical figures – one which also expresses a form of coincidence between the analogous and the contiguous – as if he were insisting on the point that it is language play which forges and takes apart the linked chains of his eternal metaphors.

In encountering Odette, the 'metamorphic adventures' of the 'little phrase' have not reached their close. A few pages later Vinteuil's Andante concludes by coming right up against the threat of mental illness which is hanging over its composer: '. . . insanity diagnosed in a sonata seemed to [Swann] as mysterious a thing as the insanity of a dog or a horse, although instances may be observed of these' (I. 234).

The 'little phrase' – in turns 'commanding' and 'liquid', 'fragrance of roses' and 'notation', 'a woman passing by' and a 'rejuvenation' of the narrator's aim of marrying an Odette who has been absorbed by the music and, thanks to the reversal of the analogy, made attractive again – comes to the end of its imaginary journeyings from metaphor to metaphor by being evoked in another little phrase: 'insanity of a dog'. These 'overprintings'[8] both irradiate and contaminate each other, depositing within each of the links of the chain the meaning of another one. By his analogical listening to music, Swann's physical love passes from confusion to sublimation and ensures its own survival. And yet the logic of Proustian overprinting already enables us to anticipate that it is over-inflated and doomed to destruction, with the tipping over of the divine into animal madness. What is it that binds these two extremes together in an ultimate metaphorical link? Is it music itself? or Swann? or Odette? The question remains without an answer, for Proust's palimpsest overburdens the message, but far from annihilating it or emptying it out, it endows it with a dramatic, unbearable, enigmatic polyphony.

Later on, the hearing of the same Vinteuil sonata at Mme de Saint-Euverte's evening party will succeed in confirming these initial metaphorical intimations. Swann discerns in it the 'charms of an intimate sadness', 'their very essence, for all that it consists in being incommunicable' (I. 379): musical form – which is hostile to any form of reasoning but, as we have seen, permeable to metaphor – achieves the status of 'actual ideas, of another world, of another order, ideas veiled in shadow, unknown, impenetrable to the human mind' (I. 379–80) and reveals to him that Odette's love for him is already dead. 'From that evening onwards, Swann understood that the feeling which Odette had once had for him would never revive.' (I. 384) No more would his love for her: what was it but an impression, a transposition? ' "To think that I've wasted years of my life, that I've longed to die, that I've experienced my greatest love, for a woman who didn't appeal to me, who wasn't even my type." ' (1.415)

Metonymy and the narrative framework

The prevalence of metaphor in Proust's imaginative world establishes, as we have just seen, connections which are purely metonymic. As Stephen Ullmann pointed out, these figures rely upon the *proximity* of two sensations, or indeed their *coexistence* within the same mental context. With regard to this feature, all the condensations of two qualities which are effected by the Proustian analogies could be said to have their basis in metonymies, since these qualities become joined together, or at least are found adjacent to one another, in the desires, daydreams and 'intelligences' of the characters and the narrator. In an even more explicit way, connections in space – the contagious effects of the sign – provide a metonymic basis for the majority of Proust's metaphors. The most striking case is the analogy, woven across thirty or so pages, between the Charlus–Jupien couple and the fertilization of the Duchess's orchid by a bumble-bee. Charlus hums 'like a bumble-bee', Jupien stays 'implanted there like a tree', but 'at the same instant' and in the 'same place' their 'conjunction' becomes juxtaposed with the amorous coupling between the orchid and the bumble-bee, with the effect that the two couples are coexistent both in time and in space, and in the perception of the narrator. From his viewpoint, Jupien 'struck poses with the coquetry that the orchid might have adopted on the providential arrival of the bee' (II.626). What is contiguous becomes metaphoric.

Whether integrated in metaphor, or subject to its magnetic

force, metonymy is the means of establishing the Proustian analogy in space. In eliminating time, it also establishes a space. Thus the poetic impact of the analogy becomes inserted within a *framework* which can also turn into the *container of a plot*. And yet, this immanence of metonymy within metaphor is not sufficient, as has sometimes been alleged, to transform the poetic tale originally foreseen by Proust into the complex narration which *A la recherche* turned out to be. Metonymy makes the space enticing, but there is also a need of *characters* in order that the spatial framework thus set up can generate an action, with the characters going about their own modes of self-fulfilment.

What is more, the very complexity of Proust's metaphor – its contradictory, paradoxical nature – contains the germ of a form of figuration. What will be figured is precisely the type of 'psychic contraction' which we call a 'character', and in order to prove itself, character will need the *events* that bulk so large in *A la recherche* without making it in any way a suspense story.

In depth: surgeons and X-ray operators

However brief and fragmented, analogy is the technique which gives rise to the instantaneous effect, like a bolt of lightning. Analogy divides the world and the story into successive links, sometimes heavy and sometimes light, which endow the Proustian discourse with the pregnant, poetic quality of synaesthesia, and at the same time cause the intermittent effect of a multitude of still-frame presentations of the image. These sudden shocks woven into circles surprise us, leave us thunderstruck, irritated or convinced in turn: with their lining of sensation and their logic of condensation following the primary processes of the unconscious, they impose their own type of truth. *The analogical is the ontological*: Proustian metaphor brings together appearances, but it also reveals the profundity of being. Analogy passes through the visible until it achieves a 'transparent unity', where things become ranged in an order quite different from that which the intelligence necessarily imposes; they are 'converted into one and the same substance', with no 'impurity', and life acquires depths:

. . . that life of ours which cannot effectually observe itself and of which the observable manifestations need to be translated and, often, to be read backwards and laboriously deciphered. Our vanity, our passions, our spirit of imitation, our abstract intelligence, our habits have long been at work, and it is the task of art to undo this work of theirs, making us travel back in the direction from which we have come to the depths where what has really existed lies unknown within us. (III.932)

Once he is capable of perceiving things metaphorically in this way, working through intermittencies, the narrator gains access to 'some general essence, common to a number of things' which will be 'his nourishment and his joy' – 'but only at a certain depth, beyond the reach of observation'. Being quite distinct from 'observation', this *metaphorical apprehension of depths* will be compared first of all to the art of the geometrician who strips things of their sensible qualities and sees only their linear substratum: in the writer's case, this will involve a 'point that was common to one being and another', 'situated in the middle distance, behind actual appearances, in a zone that was rather more withdrawn' (III.738). But this initial analogy between writing and geometrical depth is soon supplanted by another: metaphorical depth is described in terms of surgery and X-rays:

So the apparent, copiable charm of things and people escaped me, because I had not the ability to stop short there – I was like a surgeon who beneath the smooth surface of a woman's belly sees the internal disease which is devouring it. If I went to a dinner-party I did not see the guests: when I thought I was looking at them, I was in fact examining them with X-rays. (III. 738)

This portrayal of the metamorphic imagination as a kind of surgical incision, which passes beyond 'sensible qualities' and uncovers 'the point which was common to one being and another', recalls a metaphor used by Proust in an unfinished study to describe the art of Chardin.[9] And yet the painter, whose magical light reconstitutes, in Proust's eyes, the beautiful and immediate truth of simple, worn and insignificant things, is offered to us as the very opposite of a gynaecologist. Is this a contradiction by reference to the surgeon of *Time Regained*? Not necessarily so. Chardin is presented as being at the opposite pole from the kind of gynaecologist who might have the nerve to *explain* to a woman 'the act she has had the mysterious strength to accomplish'. Chardin is on the side of the flesh; in place of the verbiage of the man of science, he immediately recalls the woman's act of giving birth: in direct light, with no explanations given. When Proust takes up the gynaecological metaphor for art once again, twenty-five years later, the narrator of *A la recherche* is no more willing than Chardin to accept the explanations of the gynaecologist. He may be keeping the same object of exploration: 'the smooth surface of a woman's belly'. But instead of seeking to provide rational explanations, he X-rays it, and this in-depth illumination which he supplies to the most intimate parts, delving below the politeness of appearances, is not essentially different from the flood of light which inundates Chardin's unsophisticated objects. The old painter and the narrator come together in the form of the ideal artist whom the young Proust had described as 'a man of keener awareness, his delight too intense, so that it overflowed into unctuous brushstrokes and immortal pigments' (ASB, 124). To go even further, the painter and the writer both participate in the lightning effect of the natural process of birth associated with woman, since all 'creative acts proceed indeed not from a knowledge of their laws, but from an obscure and incomprehensible power, which we do not make stronger by illuminating it' (ASB, 131). Chardin the artist of immediacy stays with Proust even in Venice, as when the narrator of *A la recherche*, on holiday there with his mother, finds the light of the old master mingled with the sensibility of Veronese in the blue-green tinctures of the sunshine (III. 640).

Hence, from the earliest stages of his vocation, Proust is engaged in the search for another logic which will supplant the laws of knowledge proper to ratiocination and natural science.[10] His youthful studies enable us to understand that he made a distinction between a *substantial* style – one that is capable of restoring in an instant 'the divine equality of all things before the mind that contemplates them, before the light that beautifies them', like the style of Chardin or Flaubert – and a *metaphorical* style, like that of Rembrandt, and later Elstir and Proust himself, which establishes imaginative connections and discloses the unsuspected depths of things in a way that appearances cannot.

And yet, the opposition sketched out here is hard to sustain. Is that the reason why the article on Chardin remained incomplete? It may be true that 'metaphor alone can lend a sort of immortality to a style, and in the whole of Flaubert there is perhaps not one good metaphor'. But, by contrast, Proust's close inspection of the objects illuminated by Chardin reveals, over and above their marked substantiality, their unmistakable and absolute 'associations', 'affinities' and 'friendships'. Prior to any form of appearance, therefore,

might we suppose there to be a placing together, a relationship, the sketch for an analogy?

Chardin goes further still in bringing objects and people together in
these rooms which are more than an object and than a person too
perhaps, which are the locus of their lives, the law of their affinities or
their contrasts . . . the sanctuary of their past. All here is friendship
. . . (ASB, 128)

Memory, affinity and contrast are already contained in the
most immediate of appearances; the ontological has no need
to *become* analogical, since analogy is there from the start, as a
necessary equivalent to ontology, having unquestioned sway
and establishing the necessity of art. Once there is 'imagination' – described by the narrator as being 'the only organ that I
possessed for the enjoyment of beauty' (III. 905) – there is
analogy. Being is doubtless there before us, but we can enjoy it
only by imagining it in metaphors.

And yet, to the extent that the scheme of *A la recherche*
develops and the pages of the monumental work build up,
analogy does not simply endure, extend and take hold, but its
sealed 'links', its cross-hatching of instants, become deployed
within the *action* of the novel, which may not be a picture but
is certainly a 'social kaleidoscope'. I shall return, in later
researches on Proust, to this narrative syntax, which takes
charge of the links formed by metaphors and draws them out,
in the form of their psychological equivalents which are
characters, across the enormous extent of the work. For the
moment we should notice that, just as the gynaecologist has
turned into a surgeon and X-ray operator, so the symptom has
changed in its turn: the smooth belly which, in the eyes of the
young Proust writing his commentary on Chardin, enshrined a
life in embryo, has been replaced in *Time Regained* by 'the
internal disease which is devouring it'. Here it is not merely a

question of the hypochondria of a dying man disillusioned with his Faubourg, once brilliant and now a parody of its former self. The depth at which the disease reveals itself, over and beyond the embryo, was surely a necessary factor in Proust's experience right from the start of *A la recherche*. For without this dramatic dimension of depth, which contains its appointed end, how could time have been prevented from fleeing ever onwards in search of anecdotes (like a realist novel) or dissolving into shafts of poetic brilliance (as in *Jean Santeuil*)? Proust had steered past these two sandbanks, and, in putting off his work, was waiting for the very moment in which his experience of analogy would lead him to the deep-seated sense of evil. Only from that basis could appearance and memory, spectacle and sensation, worldliness and essence be telescoped within the construction of a narrative whose metaphorical weave would be capable of extending over the cruelty of history and of society, with the writer, joyfully supported by the certainty of his vision, plying his loom with patient authority.

The essence of the world crumbles into images

We need to take one further step into the closed spiral which constitutes the metaphorical story of *A la recherche*.

If analogy, in revealing the truth of the flesh, asserts itself as ontology, ontology itself sparkles with a multitude of images. Compared with the ascetic life of the writer, *society* which is reduced to mere *worldliness* and *fashion* is no more than a spectacle, made up of appearances juxtaposed or set in contrast to each other, its only reality springing from the ephemeral decrees of public opinion. As opposed to the experience of depth, this universe of caprice (Oriane), gossip (Léonie), whim (Françoise), excommunication (Mme

[69]

Verdurin) and hidden vice (Charlus, Saint-Loup and many others) is constructed from convention and rhetoric, their forcefulness as social decrees serving only to make the world in this sense, and history itself, seem more unreal. People have often expressed surprise at the decadent snobbery, not to mention the fickle immaturity, that Proust is supposed to demonstrate by his excursions into society and by the dominant place occupied by 'the world' and 'fashion' in *A la recherche*.[11] Yet not only is the narrator in no way complicit with the views of the Faubourg Saint-Germain, but he also amuses himself in 'cracking' it: he enjoys taking X-ray images of an aristocracy which at the start exerts its own fascination, in order to show what shameful depths it conceals, just as he likes to strip the ambiguities from a seascape, a kiss or an expression of jealousy.

He does so by unfolding the likenesses, the transferences, the counterfeiting and the analogical processes; he leaps from one surface appearance to another, from one political intrigue to another, from one social cast to another. However, this decipherment of worldliness in all its modes does not bring him to an essence which would be the sole property of the social world, since it is only the essential experience of literature that appears 'divine' to him. Under the influence of metaphor, the 'essence' of the spectacle crumbles into images, appearances, acts of mimesis. The 'essence' of the world is analogy to the extent that Being is subsumed in Opinion, which is a demonic array of transferences and metaphors. In this sense, Proust's view of society, far from being old-fashioned, comes close to our own, and the elegant pages of *A la recherche* come to seem like one of the very first modern visions of the society of the spectacle. In advance of television and the media, Opinion in the Faubourg Saint-Germain, as re-created by Proust, transforms its supposed protagonists into mere apparitions, into 'looks'. Vision in depth can get beyond the pathos of love affairs, jealousies and deaths, in order to invest the social game with the universal and contagious presence of fleeting and reversible images. So is the hope of X-raying the fashionable world in search of its essence doomed to disillusionment? On the contrary, it comes to its conclusion in an ironic and jubilant finale. It is easy to imagine Proust's sardonic but obviously stifled laughter when he demonstrates that this game of social hierarchies, this stock exchange of worldly values, this gamut of alliances, misalliances and foolish claims, has no further secrets to hide. Even Sodom and Gomorrah, though still unredeemed, are thoroughly tamed and take up their places there: the 'inverts' interact marvellously well with these 'reflecting surfaces', 'reflections' and false appearances which make up the conventions of society, in terms of which the trials of their senses – like a last level of metaphor – become acknowledged and work themselves out. So is time regained in terms of metaphors of sensation, links conjoining Eros and image – and is this the End of the Story?

Yes, in one sense. For how is it possible to look into a future or project an action, when no identity will keep within its limits any longer? Oriane lets herself down by holding a salon, whilst Mme Verdurin ends up a Princess. Even vice can no longer claim to be extraterritorial. Perversion is an integral aspect of Opinion, in *Time Regained*, and everyone has one of their own, with the exception of the narrator who maintains his aesthetic ambition, the only real one, absorbing and concealing all his other 'looks'.

All that survives, then, is the intensity of passion and the rightness of artistic composition. Mauriac is quite correct to see in Proust, who distanced himself from God as well as from grace, an exemplary form of witness which has had its effect on the writers who admired him by turning them away from

Catholicism to become humanists and psychoanalysts.[12] X-raying the passions of love brings our illusions down to the level of roles which are there to hide the scorch-marks of sado-masochism. Not even the Infinite Being can escape from this awareness of dissolution: he comes across as being porous, artificial, imaginary. If the writer feels justified in competing with his creativity, he can profane it only by re-creating it; he strips it of its essential nature, appropriates it for himself and, for his part, unveils the artifice of Being. Proust's snobbery, so often denounced and irritating as it is, is perhaps just a way of revealing his awareness of the omnipresence of artifice, of showing that he belongs to the universal system of false appearances. It may seem paradoxical but it is in fact, quite clearly, through unveiling the artificiality of love and of Being, through allowing himself to be devoured by this artificiality – devoured by the World, devoured by the Work – that Proust qualifies as the most authentic of all the French writers of the twentieth century.

Is that perhaps the reason why so little reference is made to Proust, even though his fame was assured even before his death? After Proust, French literature celebrates *amour fou* with Breton and Aragon, turns into philosophy with Sartre, into politics with Malraux and morality with Camus; it strips itself down once again, in Flaubertian fashion, with the minimalism of Blanchot and the *nouveau roman*, and lastly, with Céline, it competes with the Proustian quest for emotion, but symptomatically rejects his 'Franco-Yiddish' style and his sexuality.[13] Blanchot's Orphism is exceptional in the attention that it pays to Proust, but it gives pride of place to the implosion of the vacuum that fills the sphere of *Time Regained*. Blanchot's insight must still be measured against his silence on the subject of violence and evil, which for Proust remain the inescapable reverse side of the inconsistency of

Being. It will be left to a Catholic moralist like Mauriac, curious to know the delights of Hell, and an explorer of mystical experience like Bataille, to insist upon the amoral nature of this work – the one to deplore it, the other to praise it, both of them equally admiring. But the unity of the Proustian experience – sensual, artful and blasphemous – yet escapes us.

IV
PROUST AS
PHILOSOPHER

I

'Ideas come to us as the successors
to griefs'*

The past sensation remains within us, and involuntary memory brings it to light when an experience in the present bears a connection to it. Past and present sensation are magnetized by the same desire. In this way, an *association* of sensations is established, across time and space: a link, a composition, a reminiscence of the desire. Within this interlaced network the sensation becomes fixed and turns into an *impression*: that is to say, its particularity and isolation disappear, and a resemblance is established between differences which will eventually achieve the status of a general law, in the same way as does an idea or a thought. Yet far from being an abstraction, this 'generality', which has sensation immanent within it, leads accordingly to the highest level of knowledge: *it becomes incarnate*. The process of composition, for the person in whom it 'creates new powers' and does not confine itself to 'symbolizing a call', as in the case of Swann (III.911), never loses its anchoring in the senses; music becomes a world, writing a form of transsubstantiation.

Proust never stops 'deciphering', and yet his world is not made up of 'signs'. Or at any rate, it is not made up of word-signs, or idea-signs, and even less of signifiers and signifieds. The banal signs of language disappoint him, or make him laugh (as when someone says 'Gosh!' at the shadow of a cloud on the water, or Bergotte uses his phrase 'How splendid!' or

Bloch his vulgar expression 'fffabulous' – 'this is no way of translating an impression' (III.925)). He much prefers the fluidity and indecisiveness of an 'atmosphere', a 'rush of blood', a sudden silence, and indeed of what he calls an 'adverb' which springs from the involuntary connection of two unformulated ideas, or an 'amalgam', as in Albertine's way of speaking, which cries out for 'further treatment'.

The youthful Proust is attentive to the lessons of Schopenhauer and his French disciples, and is even more strongly opposed to 'signs' and 'strict signification' (ASB, 137). He is an enthusiast, in a state of inspiration, wishing to set himself free, to come into contact with the 'lava ready to be released, and receive whatever form one wishes' (CSB, 422). Jean Santeuil can conceive of the work only as a type of 'poetry before words', a 'work of feeling', and so is up in arms against the notion of an unbridgeable gap between language and experience.[1] A sentence like, 'Look, the sky is as fine as a Turner,' spoken by a woman of fashion, conveys nothing whatsoever of the tremulous quality which the hero's sentences are aspiring to capture, in spite of his reservations about language, by associating weather, villages, roads, dust, grass and raindrops with a cascading flow of metaphors and metonymies.

Already pride of place is being given to the *impression*, which makes up for the ineptitude of *signs*. Words are valuable in his eyes only if they possess 'a power of evocation' working on our 'sensibility', if they manage to express 'the ancient and mysterious affinities between our mother language and our sensibility' and show their kinship with a sort of 'latent music' (ASB, 138).

The author of *Against Sainte-Beuve* is already in search of a form of lively, physical, expression, inimical to the passivity of the well-policed sign: 'the vigorous and expressive language of our muscles and our desires, of suffering, of the corruption or the flowering of the flesh' (ASB,139). The accents of romanticism can be detected here, distancing the writer not only from semiology but also from Platonism,[2] and relating him to a 'philosophy' of the dynamic and the instinctual: 'It is not through philosophical method, it is through a sort of instinctual power that Macbeth is in his own way a philosopher.' (ASB,137)

Yet the writer still has need of *a certain intelligence*. What might it be? In the beginning was suffering. People whom we love necessarily make us suffer. The sole recourse that we have in the face of this inevitable affliction is the art of living, which is indeed dependent on a special form of intelligence. It consists in being able to regard the person who tortures us as a 'reflection', 'fragment' or 'stage' of an Idea, a 'divine form': in other words, as a type of 'divinity'. Over and beyond the accidents of our unhappiness, as if we were a victim submitting to the torturer, the vision of this archetype can serve as a source of joy. In fact, if a particular grievous event that deeply affects my feeble self enables me to discern a general law governing both beings and the world, I rejoice in my discovery which is the very same thing as my art. Art alone is capable of taking its point of departure from the painful and the sordid, of building up a character of universality and thus of 'joyously peopling our life with divinities' (III.935). In this light, it can be understood that 'happiness alone is salutary', but at the same time, 'it is grief which develops the powers of the mind'. 'Grief ends up by killing' if we do not manage to extract an 'idea' from it (III.943-4). With generous irony, Proust concedes that some people may be talented enough not to have to pay the price of suffering. Alas, in his own case, the painful withering away of his body becomes a talent imposed on him, which can only contribute to his work.

'Ideas come to us as the successors to griefs.' Taking up the relay of the sufferings which give rise to them, ideas have the capacity to relieve us of the harm done by actions. And here we find that our narrator, who has turned into a psychoanalyst without warning, recovers some of the mischievous spirit of his student days as a philosopher. How can this be so? Surely the idea must be the first of all elements. We must keep faith with Plato! So Proust hesitates: 'grief is merely the mode through which certain ideas make their first entry into us' (III.944). And, moreover, there are different kinds of ideas – 'some of them from the very first moment are joys' (III.944).

This confused situation concerning which comes first, ideas or the experience of grief, is far from being resolved in the paragraph in question. Yet the narrator cannot repeat too often that 'these materials for a work of literature . . . had come to me, in frivolous pleasures, in indolence, in tenderness, in unhappiness, and that I had stored them up without divining the purpose for which they were destined' (III.935). Abandon yourself to your 'instinct', go over these 'childish nothings' once again, let yourself catch *impressions* by means of them. You will gain from them the sense of something 'renewable'; in a short time you will recollect only the general, the 'psychological law' that governs other people, 'however stupid and absurd they may have been' (III.937).

So, in contrast to what has been alleged, it is not 'signs' but 'impressions' that Proust seeks out and deciphers. These are to be found in 'myself' and by illuminating them in 'their depths' I can get away from the form of 'direct enjoyment which is incapable of giving birth to them', since it makes me vacillate, strips me of reality and infiltrates me with nothingness. I can capture the perceptible only 'after the event', going beyond the disillusionment inflicted by 'material enjoyment' and 'effective action' (III.911). The obscure form of the impression has entered into me by way of my senses, and yet it inscribes 'under the signs' and 'images' (for example a cloud, a triangle, a church-tower, a flower or a pebble) 'something quite different', in 'hieroglyphic characters' (III.912). As early as *Swann's Way* the narrator was impelled, by an 'inhibition in the face of sadness', 'to observe, breathe and attempt to go along with a level of thought over and beyond images and smells'; he was on the look-out for 'those *impressions* of form, perfume, or colour' that could not be reduced to an 'intellectual value' or to an 'abstract truth', yet still succeeded in 'building up in my mind' beyond the 'direct experience of reality', and gave rise to an 'unreasoning pleasure', 'a sort of fecundity' (I.195). At a later stage, the art of Elstir will be regarded as an authentic return to the roots of the *impression*, representing as it does 'one thing by that other for which, in the flash of a first illusion, we mistook it' (II.435). Besides the implied reference to impressionism, this flash of the Proustian *impression* which takes one thing for another can be seen in this context as another word for metaphor.

Are we concerned here with a basis of 'thoughts' and 'reminiscences' which lies beyond the world of phenomena, in the traditional style of Plato's logic? That is true to a certain extent, but the reminiscences are all of a hybrid, sensory type: 'the kind evoked by the sound of the spoon or the taste of the madeleine, or those truths written with the aid of shapes for whose meaning I searched in my brain' (III.913). *Sense-hieroglyphs* or *figured truths*, the impressions always take the form of 'complex abracadabras', of palimpsests, with the Greek idea supplying just one thread among many others.

Even the most clear-sighted reader allows himself to be taken in by Proust's declarations in praise of a 'so abstract, so ideal existence' which takes him back to the springs of the Vivonne. But through all the 'ideas' and 'signs', he is still searching for the *interweaving of impressions*. Even the airy

[81]

speculations aroused in him by the name of the *Guermantes* have their being initially in a 'hieroglyph' – a 'tapestry' as 'in the *Crowning of Esther* in our church'; a 'stained-glass window' like the one of Gilbert the Bad, ranging from cabbage green to plum blue; the 'magic lantern' which displays the ghost of Geneviève de Brabant; or indeed 'the amber light which glowed from the resounding syllable: *"antes"*' (I. 187). In his magnificent reading of Proust, Gilles Deleuze puts the accent on the way in which these signs inflict a dematerialization on the real people to whom they refer, and he sees this as the proof of Proust's Platonism.[3] Certainly the 'ducal person' of the Guermantes family becomes 'immaterial' by virtue of the criss-cross of impressions which take it over; but this derealization of persons is precisely the most effective way of opening up their limits to find room for the whole 'Guermantes way' – 'the course of the Vivonne, its water-lilies and its overshadowing trees' (I. 187). *The impression is associative and situationist*: it blurs the boundaries of the felt and the thought, just as it does those of people and the sites they belong in, confusing space and time. By depriving them of their identity, it annihilates them; but by restoring them to places and durations beyond measure, it gives them back their life, resuscitating them in those 'resurrections of the memory' which transcribe a 'new truth' upon the sensations of long ago. As such a 'strange contradiction testifying to the way in which survival and nothingness are intermingled in me', the impression bears the traces of death: 'supernatural graphics', 'mysterious groove', at one and the same time like the writings of the ancient Thoth, god of the dead, and of the hieroglyph. But the Proustian impression, going far beyond this invocation of the Egyptian precedent, has to be recognized as being grafted in the actual body of the narrator: this is so imperative that the reader has to be envisaged as undergoing the same orgasmic experience when he, too, reaches the end of *A la recherche* . . . For the Proustian narrator even in the passage recalling the death of his grandmother, the impression is there to 'refract the agonizing synthesis of survival and annihilation . . . in the organic and translucent depths of the mysteriously lighted viscera' (II. 787).

2

Being as will and
society as hypnosis

Registered in the Faculty of Law in 1890, Proust began a degree in literature in 1893, then received permission from his family to undertake a degree in philosophy in 1894. With his friends Gregh and Brunschvieg from the Lycée Condorcet, he followed the classes of Emile Boutroux on Kant, V. Borchard on ancient philosophy, V. Egger on psychology and logic, Paul Janet on philosophy and sociology, and the aesthetics course of G. Séailles. In 1894–5, Mme Proust selected as her son's private tutor his old philosophy teacher, Alphonse Darlu. Maurois cites Proust's answer to a questionnaire from 1895: 'Who are your heroes in real life? 'Answer: M. Darlu and M. Boutroux.' Yet this juvenile enthusiasm appears to have diminished with time, for in 1908 Proust states: 'No one ever had as much influence over me as Darlu and I have realized that it was bad.' All the same, it would be wrong to under-emphasize the formative effect on a young mind of a rationalist and empiricist like Darlu, who taught his pupils the morality of the Gospels from a point of view in which lay attitudes and those of fideism were intermingled, and preached the cause of social justice.[4] The notes which Proust took on his courses show Darlu for his part heavily indebted to the teachings of Lachelier in his book *Fondement de l'induction*. Sharing Lachelier's hostility to Schopenhauer, Darlu himself was however a follower of the ideas of

Ravaisson, who states that beauty is an exclusive truth and assimilates Being to power, and power to thought seeking to become conscious of itself.[5] While he escapes from the constraining effects of Darlu's moralism – which would hardly have been congenial to the future writer – Proust is already benefiting from having come into contact with a philosophy which the Sorbonne will confer upon him even more generously: one concerned with will, sympathy, the power of ideas, duration and teleology.

This philosophical tendency, which dominates the later nineteenth century in France, was ultimately inspired by German romanticism, and in particular by the Schopenhauer of *Die Welt als Wille und Vorstellung* (*The World as Will and Idea*; 1819). Lachelier and Bergson are reluctant, in the political context of the 1890s, to admit their German debt. Ravaisson, by contrast, makes no secret of it and, following the track of *The World as Will*, is never weary of debating which have primacy, sensations or judgments, what is the essential sensibility of the genius, and how the genius achieves an osmosis with the forces of nature, whose truth art succeeds in revealing.

But for Proust, experience can no more be reduced to the thought of Schopenhauer than it can to Plato, as Curtius and Deleuze would have it. The brilliant and valuable research on Proust's philosophical background leaves us in no doubt that the German philosopher was important for the young writer, and indeed for the narrator of *A la recherche*. But it is futile to put forward a Schopenhauer–Schelling straitjacket in which Proust is supposed to have been imprisoned throughout his life.[6] It is enlightening to discover that Proust's intellectual experience is specific to him, and repays studying as such, quite separately from the philosophical ground which nourished it.[7] This does not, of course, alter the fact that (as it is very difficult to isolate something as specific as Proust's 'philosophical system') the major lines of development which we have tried to follow in terms of the author's own formulations reveal on the one hand that Schopenhauer, by way of Séailles, was massively influential on him, and on the other that he had a remarkable amount in common with the lucid writings of Gabriel Tarde.

Through Hartman, Wagner and Nietzsche, Schopenhauer's thought filtered into France from 1880 onwards. But it was probably the authority of Barrès – himself the pupil of Brudeau, Schopenhauer's translator and a vigorous exponent of the terminology of the *World as Will* – that finally succeeded in captivating a young student of literature like Proust, and in securing his interest in the classes at the Sorbonne. What, then, would he have come across, in the filtered Schopenhauer taught at these classes? First and foremost, the omnipresence of *Will* as an effective and dynamic essence inherent both in the cosmos and in the individual. Intuitive Ideas, as opposed to the concepts developed by the intelligence, have direct access to this essential *Will*. Schopenhauer writes:

I consider every force of nature as a will . . . The concept of will is the only one, among all the possible concepts, which does not have its origin in the phenomenon, in a simple intuitive representation, but comes from the very foundation, from the immediate awareness of the individual, in which he recognizes himself, in his essence, immediately, without any form, even that of subject and object, it being expected that here the knower and the known coincide.[8]

Being inherent even in inorganic nature, the Will is universal: 'both here and there the name of Will is the means by which I designate the essence of all things, the foundation of all phenomena'.[9] Of this universal Will, the Idea constitutes the 'eternal form'; it is 'the immediate objecthood of the Will'.

If such an Idea succeeds in offering itself to anyone, that person 'ravished in contemplation of it is no longer an individual . . . but is the pure knowing subject'.[10] 'Ideas are in their essence intuitive',[11] and there is 'an adequate objectification of the Will'.[12]

Pure forms of a universe endowed with mutability and affectivity,[13] these Ideas of Schopenhauer have nothing whatever to do with the eternal and immutable essences of Plato, although their common terminology (inherited from Winckelmann) has often led to confusion. Schopenhauer's Ideas are coincident with the universal Will, and, just like the dynamism and creativity inherent in Nature, they are active, restless and contradictory. Only the artist is able to gain access to them, through intuition, by raising himself above individual awareness and so identifying himself with the motion of natural affectivity. But of all the arts, only *music* is capable of assimilating this forceful structuring of the world in all its immediacy. In its rhythm, and the fluidity of its harmony, it directly models itself on the Will. Thus music succeeds in being at one and the same time the Idea and essence of the world, the perfect language of Being which escapes from the 'grievousness of time': '[Music] expresses not the phenomenon but the internal essence, the inside of the phenomenon, Will itself . . . The essence with no accessory . . . flesh and blood.'[14] All the other arts – painting, sculpture and poetry – simply represent fugitive phenomena: enslaved by mimesis they are caught up on 'the wheel of time' and can but *reproduce* the dynamic structure of the 'objects' they represent, without ever being *directly* the structure of Will.

Allegory none the less benefits from Schopenhauer's indulgence. He has nothing to say in favour of pictorial allegory, which sadly diverts the spectator's mind from the visible and intuitive image to lead it in the direction of an abstraction, brings the Idea down to the level of a simple concept and so can be related to a kind of useless hieroglyphics.[15] By contrast, allegory *in poetry* offers us a concept directly in the form of words, and yet at the same time rises above the concept, summoning up an 'intuitive representation'. Here Schopenhauer evokes the logic of rhetorical tropes, and it is easy to spot the idea of the vitalist metaphor, linking meaning and sensation in the circular structure of a transposition, which proved to congenial to Proust. What is more, Schopenhauer himself generalizes with regard to the capacity of poetic allegory to raise itself to the level of the essential Will of the Idea and the World; he extends it 'to all forms of figured expression, metaphor, comparison, parabola and allegory'. The world of the baroque imagination, which is full of figures, supplies him with persuasive examples of this power of allegory to attain the essence, as in the *Criticón* of Baltasar Gracián y Morales, *Don Quixote* and *Gulliver's Travels*.

Despite the primacy of music, the poet also has the capacity to 'embrace the Idea' by way of the figures of rhetoric: he can reach 'the essence of humanity, beyond all relations, beyond time; in a word, he can grasp the adequate objectivity of the object in itself, at its highest level'.

No one is more ready than the melancholy Schopenhauer to denounce the actual powers of the world and take refuge in a Republic of Genius, to pass beyond the history of Western philosophy and open himself up to the revelations of the Vedas and the Upanishad. Since the will to live engenders suffering, in his terms, the only way out for the human spirit is engulfment in the non-self, in nothingness, 'the absolute cessation of will'. This celebrated pessimism – a response to a dislocated world, cutting right across the previous century's blithe confidence in progress – probably finds an echo in the gloomy world-view of Proust. Yet it is above all Schopenhauer's apologia for the work of art as a form of consolation, a provisional source of comfort (*Quietiv*), that will attract the attention of the writer who tenaciously holds that his work has therapeutic, if not resurrective, powers: 'Ideas come to us as the successors to griefs.' (III.944) Amongst the French philosophers of his time, Proust seems to stand out precisely in his recognition that art possesses the power to reveal and measure up to the Will of the world. Making literature in the spirit of Schopenhauer's definition of music is both the initial and the ultimate goal of his work, even though in the interval he succumbs to the 'weakness' of getting tied up in the details of phenomena, and associates painting with the model of aesthetic genius that is to prefigure the literary aesthetic of *A la recherche*.

It was through taking the aesthetics course of Gabriel Séailles – referred to in the 1894–5 session as 'Studies of sensibility' and based on ideas developed in his thesis of 1883, *Essay on the Genesis of Art* – that Proust would have been able to gain familiarity with these theories, and with their context in romanticism, which goes back to the Jena circle of Schiller, Schlegel and Schelling. He would have learned there of the apotheosis of art and the 'aesthetic enthusiasm' which, far from proving a diversion from the truth which in the Socratic tradition can be attained only through philosophy, is on the contrary the means of linking human consciousness to the natural world. This is the form of genius which Séailles celebrates. His writings show innumerable parallels with ideas developed by Proust in the course of his life. To start at the beginning, the poetry which exists 'before words' and is the goal of Jean Santeuil seems to have been directly anticipated in Séailles. But even as late as the last pages of *Time Regained*, Proust's aesthetic programme is still concerned with making explicit – in terms very close to those originally used in

Séailles' work – the idea of a *natura naturans* which is in operation everywhere but can be grasped only through the idea of the artist.[16]

In terms of this logic, a relatively insignificant place is allotted to the role of *memory*: it is confined to being a mere 'intermediary', an instrument which gives rise to sensation. We must look at another work from the time of Proust's youth, Théodule Ribot's *Psychology of the Feelings* (1897), in order to appreciate the way in which contemporary philosophy emphasized the importance of reliving memories. In this source, the abstract notion of associationism is contrasted with the genuine association, based on feelings and emotions, between memories.

Thus the philosophy of Proust's time allows the emergence of a notion of involuntary intelligence that imaginatively articulates the sensibility wherein the depths of memory are to be found. Séailles shows how this process works in painting: the image enables sensation, which is a constituent of the world, to transform itself into an element of thought. A form of unconscious operation structures the *infinite* in terms of *images*. Is this not the essential dynamic of the *Proustian sentence*? Is it not the very fusion between body and mind, nature and thought, which Proust strives for in his *impressions*? The 'secret life' of a person is already their novel: this exists 'from all eternity in the brain of a man, and certainly it has been there already on the pages where, with the aid of that sort of sympathetic ink which is thought, it is traced out again'.[17]

Memory is but the servant of imagination: it performs an alchemical role in soldering the reality of things to their spiritual equivalent. Proust looks to the philosophy derived from Schopenhauer, and not directly to Bergson, about whose ideas he remains reticent, in order to find confirmation of the pivotal position which he allots to memory. Thus in Egger's *The Interior Word* of 1881 it is explicitly stated that the subject is outside representation and finds itself in duration: the self is duration, the non-self is extent. 'The unextended which endures is the self.' By running through duration, reminiscence can bring the subject and the world together, uniting duration and extent – that is to say, existence. The original division and all subsequent oppositions are therefore transcended by what Egger calls 'reconnaissance' and Proust 'reminiscence'. Involuntary as it is, memory conceived in this way is not an internal property of the psyche: it aids the complex dynamics of the imaginary process whose role is to reconcile genius with the structuring of life.

We can now appreciate more easily Proust's reluctance to consider himself, and be considered, a clever psychologist. 'As it is a question of psychology,' he states in objection to the interpretations of Jacques Rivière, 'I can say that life, not psychology, was my goal.' How could anyone be more clear? Memory in Proust takes as its goal neither more nor less than the containment of life in the self, and the reciprocal move-ment of the self into life.

The philosopher Egger gave Proust an extremely favourable report: 'What's more, intelligent, understood everything.'[18] But in 'understanding everything' Proust's intelligence did not confine itself to borrowing from his philosophy teachers the notion that memory is the intermediary in the formation of the architectonics of imagination, and so enables the artist to communicate with the essence of Being. Often the writer is sceptical enough to question the capacity of words to reveal the 'true world' to us, let alone that of the senses (and *sight* most obviously), together with the imagination as a whole, when he singles them out for discussion: 'names are whimsical draughtsmen', whilst 'our senses [are] little more endowed than our imagination with the art of portraiture – so little, indeed, that the final and approximately lifelike pictures which we manage to obtain of reality are at least as different from the visible world as that was from the imagined' (I. 590).

Even more duplicitously, Proust combines the sacredness of music with the perversion of eroticism. Hardly has he praised the art of Wagner and the completely 'internal', 'non-factitious' power of music, which is 'hence part of life and not of logic', than the narrator makes a 'sharp turn' and associates the violin with the vicious character of the violinist Morel (III. 159). Vulgar and deceitful, Morel abruptly cuts across the sublime apprehension of music which the Schopenhauerian narrator has just favoured us with: in his vulgarity or cruelty, he cheats on the friendless Baron de Charlus with his trumped-up 'algebra lessons', and eventually the narrator surprises him berating a whore in his 'coarse peasant accent': '*grand pied de grue! grand pied de grue!*' (III. 161). The contrast with *Tristan* is a piquant one! Proust delights in establishing a 'profound union between genius . . . and the sheath of vices . . . as had happened in the case of Vinteuil' (III. 265). Nor can we possibly resist transposing this contagious relationship between vice and genius into the circumstances of Swann's cherished hearing of Vinteuil's little phrase at the Verdurins', with the entirely formal, vertical line of the violin resonating (if we read the book backwards, as it were) with all the perversity which Morel is to exhibit in *The Captive*. Yet another link is added to the metamorphic adventures of this sonata, which are indeed interminable.

Thus Proust counteracts, if he does not entirely shatter, the romantic tendency to place music in an ideal, separate realm, and roots it in the dramas of eroticism, giving it a completely human face. Art is shown to have a dual nature. On the one hand, it participates in the 'vanity' and 'nothingness' of life –

'the appearance of real individuality achieved in works being due simply to the *trompe-l'oeil* effects of clever technique'. But, on the other hand, the subtle differences between the 'reddish septet' and the 'white sonata' are a revelation of 'unsuspected universes', that 'lost homeland' with which the musician remains 'unconsciously in tune': they suggest that art is perhaps not quite so unreal as life itself. The septet is the carrier for the narrator's love of Albertine, just as the sonata was identified with the love of Swann for Odette. It is by getting erotically contaminated in this way, weighed down with jealousy, betrayal and death – and therefore at the other end of the scale from the romantic Sublime – that music qualifies itself to express the communication of souls which took place before language: 'a possibility that has come to nothing' and leaves behind only 'humdrum reality', with 'too insipid' people (III. 260–1). Deviating from the romantic interpretation, Proust none the less appropriates it for himself and saturates it with the intensity and inanity of sexual drama. Which is to say that he subordinates his philosophical borrowings to the forcefulness of his blasphemous sensibility and the excessiveness of his style. And finally, by incorporating the reverberations of the story within consciousness, he arranges for involuntary memory to dissolve into fragments – 'the intermittencies of the heart'.

For those who are able to spend more time looking into the question, Anne Henry's excellent book *Marcel Proust, théorie pour une esthétique* (1983) details the other philosophical exchanges that nourished Proust's philosophy and aesthetics: those with Ruskin, with Wilde and with Bergson. One finding is worthy of special note, since it forms a counterpoint to the essential teleology of art which is perfectly summed up by Schelling's phrase – and seems to be so relevant to the perpetual flow of metaphors and expressions in Proust: 'The fundamental character of the work of art is unconscious and infinite.'

The thinker in question is one whose analysis of social ties strikes us as specially pertinent to the society of our period. As opposed to Marx and the other sociologists who considered that society was based upon the necessity of fulfilling needs, Gabriel Tarde (whose manuscripts were entrusted to Darlu for classification) envisaged society as a cultural fact, involving ritual, convention and imitation.[19] Furthermore, he saw the protagonists in this ceremony as being manipulated by a logic which was not under their control, and which appealed to their most regressive states. In diagnosing this kind of generalized somnambulism, he obviously recalls the demystification of our psychic lives that Freud was just about to undertake. The herd-like character of social groupings, with its basis in *imitation*, is uncompromisingly brought to light, together with the need to *believe* which a whole host of religious, ideological and media-based manipulations have brought to the surface more forcefully than ever before. In Tarde's view, we are governed, on the one hand, by an implacable heredity, and on the other by the desire to be *like*, to *imitate*, to *believe in common*. 'The universality of imitation is the essential fact of social life,' writes Tarde.[20] Freedom, in consequence, starts by a process of 'de-assimilation' with regard to the group.

The disillusioning spectacle of Proustian society, which is woven from mimetic processes and foolish beliefs that cancel one another out, lends support to these suggestions. Though he is by no means a simple illustrator of sociological theory, Proust's notion of the imaginative life of society forms part of a whole current of thinking which includes the important and unjustly neglected factor of French sociology at the end of the nineteenth century. As he troops from one salon to another, the narrator recalls, obviously, the *naïveté* of the new recruit, but he also puts us in mind of the fragile irony inherent in the position of someone who, as a Jew and a writer, views society as a stranger only in order to see it as it is, in its falsity. 'Our social personality is a creation of the thoughts of other people.' (I. 20) Right at the start of *Swann's Way*, this is the diagnosis. A little later: 'Our social existence, like an artist's studio, is filled with abandoned sketches in which we fancied for a moment that we could set down in permanent form our need of a great love.' (II. 404) The Guermantes family, faithful to Versailles, and to Saint-Simon, excel in appearances: Oriane, 'who had scarcely a penny to her name, created more stir with her clothes than all the Courvoisiers put together' (II. 464). Quite naturally, they practise 'that aberration, peculiar to the life of the court under Louis XIV, which transfers the scruples of conscience from the domain of the affections and morality to questions of pure form' (II. 453). Be it another's creation, the sketch of an abandoned work of art, or pure form, our social role is for Proust the result of a conventional situation: the game has its own rules, its own rhetoric.

Our provisional, and hopefully not too schematic, conclusion is that the immense cathedral of *A la recherche* resonates with two philosophical tonalities: those of Schopenhauer and Tarde. On the one hand, there is the post-romantic wish for an imaginary life which will merge with the essence of Being; on the other, the need to X-ray the social bond as a form of imitation, to see belief as hypnosis. A good part of the fascination which Proust holds for us is due to this paradoxical conjuncture.

In the first case, imagination is a form of revealed will, the essence of Being, which ensures that experience is soundly based as it appeases the desire for power. If I can accede to Being through my imagination, then beyond the self who thinks, and with the aid of sensation, *I* is *Everything*. The will to power is fulfilled in the excesses of a jubilatory pantheism, involving sadness and enthusiasm, glory and blasphemy. Yet at the same time, and in the second case, the Being which has been captured in this way is also the site for the stage effects of Opinion, that is to say, of society which comes apart in a welter of competing images. The social bond is a mere tracing, an imitation, a process of sleep-walking; on the social stage, every will to power, whether rooted in psychology, love or the politics of small groupings, or larger ones, breaks up and disperses like a mirage. The social bond is an illusion: belief is lasting hypnosis.

At the confluence of these two streams, where Schopen-hauer and Tarde collide, Proust is able to satisfy our need for an overall view, while frustrating any tendency to social megalomania. Within a framework of metaphor and phrase which guarantees our experience of joy – as it passes from words to memories and finally to fully materialized sensations – he can disabuse us of the forms of paranoia which lead us to put our trust in strong social values. There remains one thing sacred: art. But art is not social. It shreds the social order into little pieces. In its anti-social vocation, Proust's art has only the enjoyment of Being to compete with. Face to face with the World's Will, the subject can open up his limits, impregnate himself, objects and people and, in trying to grasp hold of them, feel himself bit by bit merged in unity with them. The imaginary impression of being at one with Being as Will is based in projective identification and utilizes the latent para-noia within each person. But this is stabilized and sublimated precisely by being framed within the field of imaginative experience. There a special value is attached to the shock registered by the senses and the psyche in contact with nature, as it is to the special form of shock to our perception which is provided by the erotic. But the dividends no less than the narcissistic wounds produced by social conflict are classed as inessential phenomena.

In renouncing Being and espousing the will to social power, joy ceases to provide a possibility of rebirth for the subject and becomes alienated as a structural element. Whether he be master or slave, man's inner being thus becomes shrunken; he closes himself to experience and becomes the stake of the forces of production, of capital and the overproduction of images. So the road lies open to compromise, and abjection.

Following the extremists of the French Revolution and the Terror, the German successors to the romantic generation modified the will of and for Being into a will for power over Opinion. Thus, for them, Being became reduced to society and the subject degenerated into a relationship of the dominating and the dominated, the persecuting and the persecuted. Psychosis – which had remained fluid beneath the surface in the experience of reconciling the psyche with nature, the inside with the outside, the self with the cosmos – hardened, in the light of this reduction of experience to the social level, into feelings of insecurity amongst like groups, of being threatened by one's own kind, and into vengeful feelings towards one's own kind who are now classed as foreign. Pantheism has been miniaturized in the form of a chessboard of conflicting parties. As technical progress has succeeded in bringing about humanity's will for power over nature, so the thirst for domination over others has taken root in all the totalitarian systems of our century, not to mention a good number of artists who have failed to distinguish inner experience from the will to power in society.

Since the First World War, and even more clearly since the Second, the pleasure principle has abandoned its romantic site in *natura naturans* and has acquired the dangerous form of a will to power in society over Opinion. Taking on political, ideological, sociological and philosophical hues, literature has in its turn tried to make and unmake the social bond. Can it really get away from it? It thinks so. There is, however, no alternative position for it to take. What is the other side of Opinion? It looks as though we do not have one. In fact, what would be the Méséglise Way that we could set here as the alternative to the Guermantes Way? Religion puts itself forward to occupy this place, and in effect it often works as a principle of metaphysical balance which can set off the otherwise all-powerful weight of the religion of society and politics, as with Mauriac, Montherlant and Bataille. Then there is phenomenology, as with Sartre, which brings human experience down to the poverty-stricken level of the absurd and reduces joy to nausea.

Might Proust be the only person to keep his options open: keeping us lucid and even ironic in the face of Opinion, while at the same time leaving us immersed in the grace of Being? With him, historical time does not pass us by, but it is pointless. We have however all the space of the timeless to enjoy these sensory reminiscences, which challenge us to go beyond our limitations and glimpse Proust's 'flash of lightning' (III. 905).

So 'little Proust' is preserved from the political compromises which tarnished the lustre of so many writers and philosophers in our century, though they apparently had many advantages over him. This snobbish, fashionable, sickly individual managed to preserve, just because of all of this, his cult of art — art as a cult. It is all too easy to see how this may disappear in its turn. Belief in art? In reading? But whom do we read? Still, the cult of art might be the least, the most childlike, of illusions, the most 'natural' form of sleep-walking to offer an abiding guarantee of the life of the psyche.

Notes

Foreword

The following works are mentioned as examples of Proust criticism: G. D. Painter, *Proust: a Biography* (London, Chatto & Windus, 1959–65), 2 vols; Gérard Genette, 'Proust Palimpsest' (1961) and 'Proust and Indirect Language' (1969), trans. Alan Sheridan, in *Figures of Literary Discourse* (Oxford, Blackwell, 1982); Genette, 'La Métonymie chez Proust', in *Figures* III (Paris, Le Seuil, 1972); Genette, *Narrative Discourse*, trans. Jane E. Lewin (Oxford, Blackwell, 1972); Paul de Man, *Allegories of Reading* (Newhaven, Yale, 1979), pp. 13–16, 57–78; Hayden White, 'The Rhetoric of Interpretation', *Poetics Today* 9:2 (1988), pp. 252–74; Leslie Hill, 'Proust and the Art of Reading', *Comparative Criticism* yearbook, 2 (1980), pp. 167–85; Gilles Deleuze, *Proust and Signs*, trans. Richard Howard (London, Penguin, 1973).

Reference is also made to the following works by Julia Kristeva: 'The Ruin of a Poetics', trans. Vivienne Mylne, in S. Bann and J.E. Bowlt, *Russian Formalism* (Edinburgh, Scottish Academic Press, 1973); *Powers of Horror*, trans. Leon S. Roudiez (New York, Columbia, 1982); *Tales of Love* (New York, Columbia, 1989).

René Girard's writing on Proust and narcissism is to be found in *Things Hidden since the Foundation of the World*, trans. S. Bann and M. Metteer (London, Athlone, 1987).

Preface

1 Cf. *The Criterion*, 1922–39 (reissued by Faber & Faber, London, 1967). Curtius's 'On the Style of Marcel Proust' was published in vol. II, no. 7, April 1924 (reissue, pp. 311–20),

and 'The Death of Albertine' in vol. 11, no. 8, July 1924 (*reissue*, pp. 376–94).

2 Valerie Eliot, ed., *The Letters of T.S. Eliot* (Faber & Faber, London, 1988), vol. 1, p. 539.

3 Ibid., p. 591.

I

1 Marcel Proust, *Correspondance*, ed. Philip Kolb (Paris, Plon, 1970–83), vol. IX, p. 163.

2 Cf. M. Bardèche, *Marcel Proust romancier, Les Sept Couleurs* (Paris, 1971), vol. I, p. 204.

3 Victor Hugo, *Oeuvres complètes*, Poésie II (Paris, Laffont, 1985), p. 412: 'A Villequier'.

4 Proust, *Correspondance*, Proust to Mme Catusse, vol. X, p. 215.

5 Ibid., vol. V, p. 238; vol VI, p. 28: letters to Maurice Duplay cited in Q. de Diesbach, *Marcel Proust* (Paris, Perrin, 1991).

6 Cf. I. 41: 'It struck me that my mother had just made a first concession which must have been painful to her, that it was a first abdication on her part from the ideal she had formed for me, and that for the first time she who was so brave had to confess herself beaten. It struck me that if I had just won a victory it was over her, that I had succeeded, as sickness or sorrow or age might have succeeded, in relaxing her will, in undermining her judgement; and that this evening opened a new era, would remain a black date in the calendar.'

7 Proust, *Jean Santeuil précédé de Les Plaisirs et les jours* (Paris, Gallimard, Bibliothèque de la Pléiade, 1971), pp. 91–2.

8 Ibid., p. 95.

9 Céleste Albaret, *Monsieur Proust* (Paris, Laffont, 1973), p. 19.

10 Ibid., p. 32.

11 Ibid., p. 30.

12 Ibid., p. 117.

13 Ibid., p. 133.

14 Ibid., p. 139.

15 Ibid., p. 140.

16 Ibid., p. 64.

17 Cf. H. Bonnet, *Les Amours et la sexualité de M. Proust* (Paris, Nizet, 1985), p. 80.

18 Quoted in Proust, *Contre Sainte-Beuve*, ed. B. de Fallois (Paris, 1954), p. 282.

19 Georges Bataille, 'Marcel Proust et la mère profanée', in *Critique*, no. 47 (1946), p. 609.

20 The last sentence of this quotation is not to be found in the Penguin Classics edition, which relies on the earlier Pléiade text.

21 Cf. Martin Heidegger, *Being and Time*, trans. J. Macquarie and Edward Robinson (London, SCM Press, 1962), pp. 383ff.

II

1 ALR, I. 695: Sketch XIII in Notebook 8 (dated 1909).

2 Notebook 6, folios 482 and 494ff., Bibliothèque Nationale (hereafter BN) NA Fr. 16646.

3 Ff. 121 and 431, BN NA Fr. 16648.

4 Cf. G. Guémar, 'Sur deux versions anciennes des "Côtés" de Combray', in *Etudes proustiennes*, II, p. 214; and Volker Roloff, 'François le champi et le texte retrouvé', in *Etudes proustiennes*, III, p. 265.

5 Cf. ALR, I. 1069–72, and Fr. Leriche, 'Une Nouvelle Datation des dactylographies du *Temps perdu* à la lumière de la correspondance', in *Bulletin d'informations proustiennes*, 17 (1986), pp. 14–20. By contrast, R. Brydges dates this typescript to summer 1910. It is to be found in BN NA Fr. 16733.

6 Proust, *Correspondance*, IX, 225; cf. ALR, I. 1118.

7 BN NA Fr. 16650, Notebook 10, f. 112; Notebook 8 also refers to 'Madeleine's tenderness' (BN NA Fr. 16648, f. 55) as being almost indissociable from the mother's reading: the mother, George Sand and Madeleine thus become fused into a single line of continuity.

8 BN NA Fr. 16754, F. 10 (1 APRIL 1913).

9 BN NA Fr. 16755 (30 May 1913) and 16757, f. 512.

10 Marcel Proust, *L'Indifférent* (Paris, Gallimard, 1978).

11 Ibid., p. 60.

12 This reminiscence of John 20:15 comes by way of Proust's reading of Ruskin (*Fors Clavigera*, Letter XII). Cf. also Luke 7:37 and John 12:1–8.

III

1 Cf. Gilles Deleuze, *Proust and Signs*, trans. Richard Howard (London, Penguin, 1973).

2 Cf. André Maurois, *A la recherche de Marcel Proust* (Paris, Hachette, 1949), p 271.

3 Philip Kolb, ed., *Choix de lettres* (Paris, Plon, 1965), p. 195. Cf. also Genette, 'Proust Palimpsest'.

4 In France, rhetoric was coded by Dumarsais (1676–1756) and by Fontanier, neither of whom understood Aristotle: their versions were taught in French schools, with little exception, up to the period of structuralism (cf. Dumarsais, *Des tropes*, Paris, Flammarion, 1988; and P. Fontanier, *Les Figures du discours*, Paris, Flammarion, 1988).

5 Cf. I. A. Richards, *The Philosophy of Rhetoric* (Oxford University Press, 1936) and Max Black, *Models and Methods* (Ithaca, Cornell University Press, 1962).

6 Cf. B. Maggiori, 'La metaphora reciproce', cited in Genette, 'La Métonymie chez Proust', in *Figures* III (Paris, Seuil, 1972), p. 54.

7 Cf. ibid.

8 The word (*surimpressions*) is taken from B. Crémieux, quoted in Maurois, *A la recherche de Proust*, p. 201.

9 'Chardin and Rembrandt' (ASB, p. 122–31).

10 Cf. also 'On Flaubert's Style' (ASB, p. 261–74).

11 Cf. Genette, 'Proust Palimpsest'.

12 Proust and Freud appear to have been the major factors in the crisis of faith which turned Jacques Rivière away from the Catholic Church (cf. François Mauriac, *Du côté de chez Proust*, Paris, La Table Ronde, 1947).

13 Cf. L-F. Céline, *Lettres à la NRF 1931–61* (Paris, Gallimard, 1991), p. 88.

IV

1 Proust, *Jean Santeuil*, p. 267.

2 Cf. Anne Henry, *Marcel Proust* (Paris, PUF, 1983), for a fine analysis of the debt of Proust to his philosophical context, and

in particular to Schopenhauer: this point is emphasized in detail.

3 Deleuze, *Proust and Signs*: Deleuze privileges the role of 'signs' and 'ideas' in Proust as having a Platonic character; in fact, it is much more likely that the 'idea' celebrated in *Time Regained* derives from Winckelmann's notion, which was taken up by Schopenhauer and his French disciples.

4 Cf. Henri Bonnet, *Alphonse Darlu, maître de philosophie de M. Proust* (Paris, Nizet, 1961).

5 Cf. Anne Henry, *Marcel Proust, théorie pour une esthétique* (Paris, Klincksieck, 1983), p. 76ff.

6 Ibid., p. 86.

7 Cf. Vincent Descombes, *Proust, philosophie du roman* (Paris, Minuit, 1987).

8 Cf. Schopenhauer, *Le Monde comme volonté et comme représentation* (Paris, PUF, 1966), p. 154.

9 Ibid., p. 162.

10 Ibid., p. 231.

11 Ibid., p. 311.

12 Ibid., p. 329.

13 Cf. Henry, op. cit., p. 48ff.

14 Schopenhauer, op. cit., p. 334.

15 Ibid., p. 305.

16 Cf. Gabriel Séailles, *Essai sur le génie dans l'art* (Paris, Baillière, 1883).

17 Proust, *Jean Santeuil*, p. 598.

18 Cf. Bonnet, op. cit., p. 77.

19 Cf. Gabriel Tarde, *Les Lois de l'imitation* (Paris, Alcan, 1890) and *La Logique sociale* (1893). For Tarde, all forms of discovery are derived from earlier imitation.

20 Tarde, *Les Lois de l'imitation*, p. 181.